THE YOUNG EQUESTRIAN

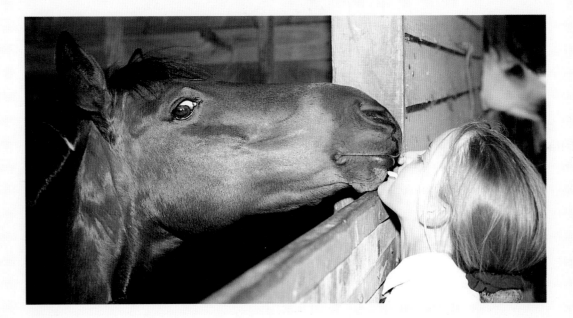

THE YOUNG EQUESTRIAN

CAROLINE DAVIS

FIREFLY BOOKS

DEDICATION

I dedicate this book to my wonderful family—to my husband Stuart, my children James and Rosemary, my parents Beryl and Keith, and my sister Rachel—and to the generous horses and ponies I have been privileged to own, care for, and ride.

A FIREFLY BOOK

Published by Firefly Books Ltd. 2000

Copyright © 2000 Quintet Publishing Limited

First Printing

Canadian Cataloging-in-Publication Data
Davis, Caroline, 1961-
        The young equestrian
Includes bibliographical references and index.
ISBN 1-55209-484-7
1. Horsemanship – Juvenile literature. I. Title.
SF309.2.D38 2000 j798.2   C00-930007-4

Library of Congress Cataloging-in-publication Data is available

Published in Canada in 2000 by
Firefly Books Ltd.
3680 Victoria Park Avenue
Willowdale, Ontario
M2H 3K1

Published in the United States in 2000 by
Firefly Books (U.S.) Inc.
P.O. Box 1338, Ellicott Station
Buffalo, New York
14205

This book was designed and produced by
Quintet Publishing Limited
6 Blundell Street
London N7 9BH

Creative Director: Richard Dewing
Art Director: Simon Daley
Design: James Lawrence
Project Editors: Sally Green and Toria Leitch
Editors: Rosie Hankin and Martin Diggle
Illustrator: Julian Baker

Typeset in Great Britain by Central Southern Typesetters, Eastbourne
Manufactured in Hong Kong by Regent
Printed in China by Leefung Asco

Contents

INTRODUCTION   6

CHAPTER ONE: WHY LEARN TO RIDE?   9

CHAPTER TWO: THE AIDS EXPLAINED   17

CHAPTER THREE: ON THE MOVE   27

CHAPTER FOUR: LEARNING TO RIDE—
                    THE FIRST LESSON   37

CHAPTER FIVE: SCHOOL EXERCISES   51

CHAPTER SIX: RIDING OFF THE LUNGE—
                    LEARNING TO WALK   55

CHAPTER SEVEN: LEARNING TO TROT   65

CHAPTER EIGHT: LEARNING TO CANTER   71

CHAPTER NINE: LEARNING TO JUMP   79

CHAPTER TEN: GOING IT ALONE   87

CHAPTER ELEVEN: HORSE CARE   97

CHAPTER TWELVE: EQUESTRIAN ACTIVITIES
                    AND COMPETING   113

                    CONCLUSION   122

                    GLOSSARY   124

                    USEFUL ADDRESSES
                    & FURTHER READING   126

                    INDEX   128

Horses and ponies have a magical quality. For some people, old and young alike, these magnificent beasts have an attraction that is almost magnetic. Throughout history, equines have played a major part in human development.

Introduction

Without equines transport, trade, and the production and distribution of necessities such as food and clothing would have been severely compromised. It is probably due to their long-standing role in human society that many humans today have a great fondness for the horse, even if they themselves do not ride or have any wish to. But for others the desire to get closer to these animals and share their world is overwhelming. It is an almost indefinable need; a need that cannot be explained in words. You have to touch horses, stroke them, groom them, care for them, and, ultimately, ride or drive them, to feel fulfilled. It is a *grande passion* that must be indulged.

While the majority of humans do not rely on equines for everyday living now, they still play important roles—as a means of making a living, to provide pleasure, and by helping some disadvantaged humans regain self-respect, enjoyment of life, and even find employment. Successful schemes include riding for the physically and mentally challenged and rehabilitation programs involving people with behavioral problems.

You do not have to be young to take up the sport of riding horses and be competent at it. For all beginners, dedication to the task in hand as well as enthusiasm, coupled with patience, care, and thought are all essential parts of the primary equation. Actually staying on a horse and directing it are the relatively easy parts for willing participants. If you lack the boldness to jump fences and "gallop with the wind," it is important to note that a quiet ride on a rented horse, with the wherewithal to control your horse in unexpected situations, is the pure essence of enjoyable riding. It is essential to realize that a person should take part in equestrian activities for his or her own pleasure, and not to please others, because this can lead to a loss of confidence and dissatisfaction.

The Young Equestrian is not aimed exclusively at young people who want to learn to ride horses; it is intended for people of all ages. Whatever your age, the capacity to learn to ride, and ride well, is there if you choose to embrace this unique sport wholeheartedly—providing you find the best possible instructor to help you share and master the delights that riding horses provides. If you have a basic level of

fitness and are "young at heart," this book will help you considerably.

As an instructor, my primary joy is opening up the special world that exists for horse and rider. I hope that this book will impress upon you the need to be patient, sympathetic, and wholly dedicated to the needs of the horses and ponies in your hands. They are dependent and reliant upon your emotions and requirements when under your control, whatever your age and whether you are a student at a riding school or an owner.

To be part of this world requires a certain amount of self-discipline. If you don't have this to begin with, you most certainly will have it before too long if equines have anything to do with it. Equines are great levelers of human pride. Whatever a person's social status, horses treat and view everyone in exactly the same way. They don't care whether a person is a prince or a pauper—but all people feel like kings when they are privileged to ride a horse or pony! In return, equines simply require that they be treated with the care and respect they deserve so they can carry out the tasks asked of them by their rider.

There is no mystery at all about learning to ride—people have been doing it for centuries. Therefore the intention of this book is simple—it is to help and encourage novice riders to master the basics of handling and riding equines with common sense and step-by-step advice and tips. For those who wish to ride competently and safely in harmony with their mount, without being put off or confused by complicated techniques and difficult terminology, I hope you will find *The Young Equestrian* helpful in achieving that aim.

Enjoy your riding.

Caroline Davis

Why learn to ride? 1

LEFT Equines, like people, love attention and want to please their owners.

ABOVE LEFT Everyone can enjoy the world of horses and horse-riding.

MIDDLE It's always fun to enter competitions, either solo or as part of a team.

RIGHT Horses love water!

BELOW As you progress you will learn first to walk, then trot, canter, and finally gallop.

To be able to ride a horse or pony safely and with regard to its comfort and well-being—both physical and mental—takes time. Even once you are competent you'll find that the learning process never stops—there is always something new and exciting to discover.

While some people may find the art of balancing on a horse at all paces easy, they may have difficulty conveying directions to the animal and understanding its intentions. Primarily it is being able to coordinate thought, intention, weight, seat, legs, and hands that people find tricky to begin with—but it does get easier with each lesson, I promise! Younger people tend to be more supple and confident than older novice riders, which can make mastering the riding process easier, but many older people possess other qualities that help enormously—patience, thoughtfulness,

determination, and empathy with the animal they are riding.

Equines, on the whole, like people, love attention, and want to please their riders and handlers. They make sociable companions and, best of all, won't judge you for who or what you are. While they cannot actually talk, they have their own unique language of noises and actions, and can make themselves understood in all sorts of ways if a person takes the time and trouble to learn how to interpret their behavior. This is the really special part of learning to ride; anyone can climb aboard a horse and ride it, but the deepest satisfaction for a true horseperson comes from understanding his or her mount, knowing what it is saying, and therefore being able to blend as one being, trusting and taking care of each other simultaneously.

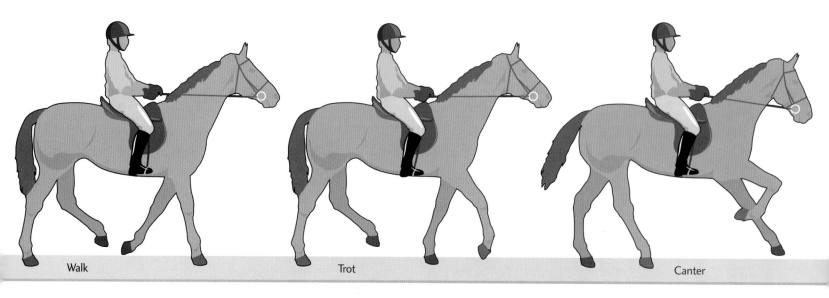

Walk

Trot

Canter

Of course you may encounter an "awkward" horse. But there was never an equine born nasty or recalcitrant; "problem" horses have been made that way by people. Once trust has been diminished by careless or cruel treatment, it can take a horse a long time to regain confidence in humans. Riding horses is one of the few sports that involves a human interacting with another living being. It is something that should not be taken up if a person's primary concern is not for the animal involved.

COMPETING

Many people have a competitive streak, and this is no bad thing because it makes you determined to try your best in whatever you do. For many riders their ultimate aim is to compete in one of the equestrian disciplines (these disciplines are covered in more depth in Chapter 12). Ribbons and trophies adorning tack-room shelves is the dream of many a horseperson, and the great thing is you do not have to be experienced to achieve that fantasy! Some riding schools put on shows for their clients, providing classes that beginners can take part in—clear round and beginner jumping (where a person can be led),

in-hand, equitation, novice dressage, and novelty classes including fancy dress are just a few examples. As a rider becomes more proficient, the choice of competitive opportunities becomes ever wider.

It is, however, important to remember from the start of your competitive career that it is the taking part that counts—not the winning, which should be viewed as a bonus. Those who strive to win, whatever the cost, invariably end up miserable when someone else is better on the day—and no one likes or respects a bad loser. A true sportsperson will concede defeat gracefully and won't blame his or her mount either. Anyone who abuses this basic code of conduct should not be associated with equines at all. Living animals are not machines and, just like humans, they can have their "off days," or misunderstand what is asked of them.

ABOVE If your aim is to be the best, there is no greater thrill than riding in competition, whatever the equestrian discipline may be.

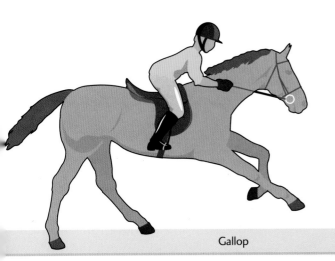

Gallop

TIME AND MONEY

Riding lessons vary in cost, depending on the school—larger establishments may be more expensive because they usually have higher overhead. It is a good idea to shop around to find the school best suited to you in terms of convenience in getting there, the price of lessons, and the qualifications and experience of the instructor. You'll find riding schools listed in the local phone book and in equestrian magazines, or ask friends who ride to see if they can recommend a school.

Choosing a riding school is often determined by its location. If you drive, then there is no problem—apart from the time and cost of fuel spent getting there, so take this into account. If you are dependent on public transport or someone else taking you, then you must check that it is convenient. For the novice rider, the major initial expenses will be the cost of lessons themselves and a helmet (the type of hat is discussed in detail in Chapter Four, along with other necessary items of clothing). Apart from these, you'll just need lots of enthusiasm!

The length of lessons for beginners varies, but no more than 30 minutes is recommended for initial sessions. It may not seem a long time, especially if you've had to travel a long way to get there, but you'll find that a half hour is plenty for your body and brain to cope with in the beginning. It is important to be on time for your lessons. Aim to arrive a half hour early for your first lesson, so that you can meet your instructor and give him or her the opportunity to assess your height, weight, and temperament in order to provide a suitable mount. Thereafter try to arrive at least 15 minutes before the lesson starts so that you start on time. If you are late, do not expect the instructor to extend your lesson time, otherwise he or she will run late for other classes.

If you cannot make your lesson, try to give the riding school at least 24 hours notice so that they can offer your booked time to someone else. Some schools will charge you the cost of the lesson if you do not give them sufficient notice. It may seem unfair, especially if your cancellation was unavoidable, but by not turning up you may have cost the school money if they were unable to fill your slot at short notice.

Real time and money expenditures come when a person decides to buy his or her own horse. While the purchase price may only be a few hundred dollars, the cost of keeping a horse can be enormous—running into thousands per year whether you keep it at home (if you are lucky enough to have the required facilities) or at a suitable boarding stable. And then there's the time factor. Will you have enough time before and after school or work, taking into account any other commitments you may have? Equines are a 24-hour, 365-day responsibility, come rain or shine, whether you feel like mucking out, grooming, and riding or not. However, if you can afford the time and money, then owning, or even sharing, your own horse can be a marvelous experience.

THE RISKS OF INJURY
AND HOW TO LIMIT THEM

Equines are living creatures and as such are unpredictable—even those that are thought to be "bombproof." Knowing how to cope competently and confidently with the unexpected is all part of the process of learning to ride and handle horses. Taking a horse for granted, especially if you know it is quiet and good-tempered, is the usual cause of a person becoming careless around or on it. This can lead to suddenly finding yourself on the floor if something startles the animal.

The biggest anxieties for novice riders are "will I fall off?" and "will it hurt?" The answers are "probably at some point" and "sometimes it will and sometimes it won't." Injuries are usually confined to being winded (although this can be quite painful and distressing for the rider at the time), the odd bruise here and there, and injured pride. The "good" thing about falls is that a rider, in most cases, doesn't actually know anything about it—one moment he or she is on the horse, the next on the floor. It happens quite suddenly and often without warning. The main thing to overcome in the first instance is the fear of falling off. If you think negatively, negative things tend to happen. If a rider is taught balance and riding and control techniques properly to begin with, the chances of falling off or becoming unseated are limited.

A well-known saying is "you are not a real rider until you have fallen off six times," but this should not be taken seriously. I have inspected the ground closely many more times than that (and expect I will do so again sooner or later) but it hasn't put me off the sport. Usually those instances have happened when I was too complacent and should have known better than to ask my mount to do something we were not properly prepared for. This in itself is a valuable lesson for a rider to learn.

Those new to the sport should satisfy themselves that the risk involved in riding is worth taking, and accept that they may encounter physical problems arising from an unfortunate, and unforeseeable, accident. However, it is worth investigating the various personal health insurance policies that are available in case of injury sustained that may result in loss of earnings and to cover the cost of medical care (see Chapter 11 for more details on this subject). Also, ensure that the riding school you patronize is properly licensed, its instructors qualified to teach (and able to administer first-aid procedure should it be required), and that it is insured against claims arising from accidents involving clients while under their tuition or simply on their premises. It is up to potential riders (or parents when

LEFT AND BELOW Riding, as with any other physical sport, has an element of risk. Happily, serious accidents are rare; the rider on the left found her fall a "refreshing" experience.

minors are involved) to check that a riding establishment fulfills its own health and safety expectations (more details on this in Chapter Four).

There are occasions when an accident occurs due to negligence on the part of a riding school or an instructor. In these cases it is in the public interest for that incident to be investigated by relevant authorities. However, bear in mind that instructors really are taking their reputation and livelihood in their own hands every time they conduct a lesson. To this end, it is important for a client to take some responsibility for his or her own actions, and as well as following a teacher's directions (which are designed to ensure safety as well as to instruct) you should be aware that you, as the client, have the power to say "no" to instructions that you do not feel confident in carrying out confidently and safely. Those people who cannot accept the possible injury risk that horse-riding carries should not take up the sport in the first place.

BELOW Riding is a sociable sport that invariably involves you meeting like-minded people and making lifelong friends.

RIDER ASSESSMENT

The beauty of people, as with horses, is that we all have different strengths and weaknesses, physical as well as mental. Both attributes play an important role in the type of rider you are or want to be.

It does not always follow that a bold and confident person will find riding easier to master than might a more timid and sensitive person. Confidence in your own abilities can be instilled with correct teaching. Sometimes a confident person finds his or her boldness can be a hindrance in that he or she cannot help trying to run before the basics of standing up and walking are absorbed. On the other hand, a more cautious person tends to think first and act later. Both attributes have their advantages and disadvantages—it is up to the instructor to temper boldness with caution, and bolster timidity with confidence.

Temperament has a great bearing on how a person rides and handles equines. A fiery person, quick to anger, will find life for both horse and rider miserable unless he or she can learn the self-discipline to be patient and calm around horses—and humans too for that matter. A person who is so laid-back as to be almost horizontal will need to "wake up"—you cannot afford to be half-asleep around equines, otherwise they'll be home long before you are, in both senses of the phrase.

Human shape and conformation can determine how easily a novice rider achieves a feeling of security and comfort on a horse (this subject is dealt with in detail in Chapter Three). While the ideal shape is to be tall with long legs, it is not a prerequisite to riding well.

HEALTH MATTERS

Riding horses provides excellent physical exercise—for physically disadvantaged people as well as the able-bodied. However it is important that those with health or physical problems consult their physician before taking up the sport to ensure that their health won't be put at unacceptable risk. Those with respiratory diseases, allergies, physical problems, and so on, often find that they can still enjoy riding, provided that their physicians' health guidelines are followed, and their riding instructors are aware of the situation and are trained to deal with unexpected difficulties should they arise.

Respiratory problems, such as asthma, can be life-threatening, so it is essential that sufferers do not put themselves at undue risk. Avoid situations where there is excessive dust and hair in the atmosphere (such as grooming dusty or molting horses). Wearing a dust mask for working around the yard can be helpful—consult your physician for advice. Those who suffer skin allergies should ensure that as much of their skin as possible is covered while they are around or riding horses.

Having to wear glasses can be a pain—sometimes literally in the event of a fall when the peak of a helmet presses down onto the nose bridge. If you wear glasses it is advisable to choose a schooling helmet as opposed to a helmet with a fixed peak. Lighter, plastic safety lenses are now available for sportspeople to wear, instead of heavier glass that can shatter if it receives a blow. It makes sense to consult your optometrist about your options. Also, wraparound glasses are more comfortable to wear than straight-sided ones that can slip down your nose. Glasses have the annoying habit of misting up when you get hot, or when the temperature rises suddenly from cold to hot. Rain, too, impairs vision. There is not a lot you can do about these problems unfortunately—except consider wearing contact lenses. They are comfortable, vision is one hundred percent improved, and there's no more misting up and peering through rain-smeared lenses. Problems only occur when hair or dust and grit get underneath the contact lenses, necessitating their swift removal.

However, the pros outweigh the cons, making these the best option.

An old injury, especially in the back or pelvic area, can sometimes be aggravated by riding and it is a good idea to consult your physician about the likelihood of this and what to do about it should it cause problems. It is also important to inform your riding instructor so that he or she is aware of a potential problem and can tailor your lessons to avoid aggravation. Wearing a surgical support on weak areas can help, but consult your physician first.

If you are severely overweight, it is sensible to lose those extra pounds first. Apart from the physical problems you may encounter, many riding schools simply do not have animals (and saddles) that are up to carrying excessive weight comfortably. Bear in mind that a novice's weight is heavier for a horse to carry until that person learns to balance and distribute his or her weight correctly.

LEARNING METHODS

First and foremost, the techniques and theory involved in learning to ride incorporate the traditional—"classical"—principles of past great horsemen and teachers, such as Xenophon, François Robichon de la Guérinière, Alexis-François L'Hotte, and Antoine de Pluvinel. The main aim, and core method, of a good riding instructor should be to teach a person to sit on and direct a horse in all paces and over obstacles—safely, confidently, and comfortably. In order for a person to achieve this, the teacher also needs to convey to the novice the importance of understanding a horse's mental and physical powers and needs so that a rider

NERVES
It doesn't matter what age you are, you are bound to experience fear while learning to ride or riding on your own. If you feel that you cannot do what is asked of you, you have the power to say "no" and ask why. A good trainer will understand your worries and want to help you overcome your fears.

RIGHT A star in the making.

BELOW Riding allows you the opportunity to be able to do things you never dreamed of, let alone thought you'd be capable of doing.

or handler may communicate effectively and sympathetically with the animal. In short, the instructor has to make a novice understand that a horse is not a machine that can be switched on and off at the touch of a button.

The core method of learning to ride consists of a person becoming familiar with equines, both inside and out. Understanding its psychology

and physiology helps enormously in the task of communicating with a horse. This is a continual learning process throughout your riding life. Balance is taught, along with the aids—signals by which a person asks a horse to do something (these are explained in Chapter Two). Balance and aids combine so that the rider then learns how to stay on a horse at halt and when it moves at all paces—halt, walk, trot, canter, and gallop— and, if a person is inclined, over jumps.

In addition to the basic core method, there are various other techniques used to enhance someone's riding ability. A few examples of these methods include the Alexander Technique (which improves balance, co-ordination, and mobility of the human body while freeing the muscular tensions that can cause tiredness, discomfort, and limited movement), training using sport psychology (by which physical performance is influenced and improved by using the mind and feelings), and TTeamwork (which involves using bodywork and ground exercises to help train horses and humans to be safe and cooperative partners). Taught correctly these methods can be extremely useful.

The aids explained 2

LEFT In order to be able to convey to the horse exactly what is required of it when it is ridden, the rider uses a co-ordinated system of natural (physical) commands, known as aids.

ABOVE Using natural aids.

"Aids" are signals conveyed to the horse by its rider to inform the animal what is required of it. It helps to know a little about them before your first lesson.

Horses have to be taught, by knowledgeable riders, to understand and respond to a traditionally used system of signals in the first place. This system has to be reasonably constant in order for riders to be able to ride different animals and still be able to communicate with them. From a horse's point of view, this is only fair because life would become pretty confusing if all its riders employed totally different systems of signals. However one country's system may vary slightly from another's, and this should be taken into account should you have the opportunity to ride abroad.

NATURAL AND ARTIFICIAL AIDS

There are two types of aid—natural and artificial. Natural (or physical) aids comprise the use of a rider's mind (mental aid), weight, seat, legs, hands, and voice, and they are used together to produce the desired reaction in a horse. Having seen proficient people ride, it looks easy to novices—until they try it for themselves and they discover that co-ordinating balance and control is no simple task! Artificial aids comprise equipment such as whips, spurs, martingales, and other various gadgets, and they are designed to enhance natural aids when necessary. However, it is important that they are not used by unknowledgeable people because their effects can be damaging and distressing to equines if misused.

Strictly speaking, a bit is also an artificial aid, and therefore great care should be employed in its use. Chosen and fitted correctly, and used sensitively to guide the animal, the lump of metal that comprises most bits will not hurt or damage an equine's mouth.

HOW TO USE AIDS

THE RIDER'S MIND

Mental aids are an important part of successful riding. Basically, your mind is the "command center" for all other aids. Never underestimate the power your mind has in helping you to achieve what you want. There is much to be said about thinking positively—generally if you set your mind to achieving an objective, you will find some way of doing it. Similarly, if you think that something cannot be done, then you tend not even to attempt it. Having a positive outlook, even when the odds are stacked against you, gives you more of a fighting chance.

Being positive helps promote confidence, and confidence in turn helps you to win through. Think about other instances, apart from riding, in which thinking positively about something has helped enormously. It could have been learning to ride a bicycle, an exam at school that you were dreading yet turned out to be not so bad, or a driving lesson or test, where trying to remember everything the instructor had told you seemed like a mission impossible but you succeeded anyway and then wondered afterward why you had thought it so difficult!

When I was about 10 years old, my teacher told me, rather bluntly, that "there is no such word as can't—if you put your mind to the task, you will find a way of accomplishing it. The end result might not be perfect, but at least you will have the satisfaction of having tried." I learned a similarly valuable lesson from a friend. Whatever her problems, whatever the weather, and no matter how difficult other people were being, she remained serene, cheerful, diplomatic, and smiling throughout. She simply never seemed to let things get her down. I found this amazing. How did she do it? When I asked, her answer was beautifully simple. She said, "Why choose to be miserable when you can choose to be happy and positive?" She was absolutely right—being positive is a much nicer, and healthier, frame of mind to be in.

But what has all this to do with riding horses? In fact, your mental outlook contributes a great deal in deciding your success in the saddle, as well as out of it in other walks of life. Imagination can be a wonderful thing when channeled positively. On horseback, a useful "mind game" to play, especially if you are a little worried about something, is to pretend you are your favorite showjumper or dressage rider. Imagine sitting as tall and proud and easily as the experts do. Their bearing and position on a horse is just so; they don't worry if a horse bucks or prances because they are confident they can sit comfortably and without fear. Unconsciously, as you imagine yourself in their position, you find yourself relaxing and suddenly moving automatically with the horse instead of against it. And the horse seems to relax too. That is the power your mind has over your body; and if you relax, so does the horse.

Equines are quick to sense fear and tension in a rider. Although riding horses are no longer herd animals in the wild, their instinct for survival is still strong, and picking up "danger signals" from other herd members was essential if they weren't to end up as another animal's meal. This is why it is important for a rider (who, in the horse's mind, is a herd member) to remain calm and relaxed at all times. This can be difficult, but being able to use your mind positively to remain calm pays dividends in taking the heat out of potentially awkward situations.

How you use your mind when riding determines the effect of your physical aids on the horse and how it reacts to them.

WEIGHT

How, when, and where a rider uses his or her weight in the saddle determines how a horse will move and react. The law of gravity dictates that a person's weight travels down from the top of the

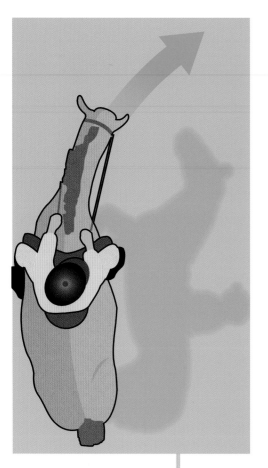

TURNING

Asking your horse to turn involves co-ordinating your mind, hands, seat, weight, and legs. Here the rider will be looking to the right; asking for a right bend in the horse's neck with the right rein; checking the amount of turn and controlling the pace with the left hand; maintaining equal weight on both seatbones; remaining straight in the saddle and not leaning into the bend; keeping the right leg on the girth to encourage the horse to "bend" around it and to provide support, and keeping the left leg just behind the girth to maintain impulsion and to stop the horse's quarters swinging out too much to the left and overbending.

head, through the body, to the ground. This is why it is important for a person to sit on a horse over its center of gravity to ensure that both are balanced and stable during movement. A horse's center of gravity is just behind the withers, but it moves around a bit depending on the pace and activity of the animal. This may seem confusing for a beginner rider, but how you remain in the right position in relation to the horse's center of gravity at all times becomes apparent when you become accustomed to riding.

In the saddle, a rider should be sitting with equal weight on each of his or her seatbones. To check this, slip your hands, palms up, under your seat and you should feel your seatbones quite distinctly. If the weight is unequal, then re-align it until the pressure on both hands is equal. Each seatbone sits on either side of the horse. Putting more weight on one seatbone takes weight off the other—with the person becoming a heavier burden to carry on one side of the horse, which can unbalance it. Think of riding a bicycle or a motorbike. If you lean more to one side, therefore putting more weight on that side, the machine will tip that way. If it tips, you will have to counterbalance it by shifting your weight momentarily to the opposite side until it rights itself, and then you would apportion your weight equally to ensure the bike remains balanced.

The same principle applies when riding a horse. To maintain your center of gravity, you need to remain tall, yet relaxed, in the saddle. It

is essential that joints remain loose and relaxed ("soft") for three purposes: To allow weight to travel down through the body; to allow the joints to function properly; and to act as shock absorbers. If a rider's body is tense and unmoving then a horse's action is quite likely to unbalance or unseat that rider.

The more weight going down into a rider's seat, legs, and feet, the more stable the seat and upper half of the body will be. To understand this principle, try this mental image: Imagine holding up a piece of string with a lump of lead attached to the bottom of it. See how the lead, being heavy, remains at the bottom and holds the string straight and steady. Now imagine your lower legs and feet as being the lead and your upper legs, seat, torso, and head being the string. Weight allowed to travel down into the legs helps stabilize them in the correct position and thus leg aids may be applied effectively.

The effect of a rider's weight in the saddle can be made heavier or lighter. A heavier seat weight generally indicates to the horse that a faster pace or more impulsion (energy) is required, while slowing down is indicated by making the seat weight lighter, although a lighter seat can, in some circumstances, be used to allow or encourage *more* forward movement, for example when galloping. For someone watching a rider alter seat weight, the movement is almost imperceptible; it is only by watching the horse's reaction that the application of a weight aid becomes apparent. The alteration is so slight, yet the horse feels it immediately. There are also instances when a rider may need to adjust light weight to heavy in order to carry out a slowing-down process correctly. This is to ensure that the horse still maintains impulsion from the hind quarters so that these do not get "left behind," for instance

in a transition (change of pace) from walk to halt. In addition, a heavier seat aid can have different effects, depending on how it is co-ordinated with the other aids, especially the rein aids.

To lighten your weight in the saddle, simply imagine that there is a piece of string attached to the top of your head which someone is pulling up ever so gently, and allow your body to follow the action of that thought. To increase your weight in the saddle, imagine that someone is gradually releasing the string's pull, and allow your body, again, to follow the actions of that image. It's as simple as that. If you look

down at your horse or the ground—common position faults which are due to negative thinking—the effect is one of making you heavier in the saddle. This is not a desirable effect if you want to slow the animal down, let alone avoid crashing into something.

Physical aids should be done imperceptibly. Watch accomplished riders in action and carefully observe how they apply aids. You won't see the best of them applying aids obviously, yet their horses respond as if by magic. Aim to create this magic yourself. Balancing position and weight correctly in the saddle is the key element in applying all other aids effectively.

ABOVE The girth area of a horse, behind the top of the foreleg, is where major leg aids are effective.

LEGS

A rider's legs help keep him or her securely mounted on a horse, and they act as the "gas pedal" or "accelerator" when the horse's pace requires adjusting. A rider uses his or her lower legs (the calves)—in conjunction with weight, seat, and hands—to ask a horse to move and maintain movement as required. This is done by positioning the legs in certain places on and around the animal's girth area and by squeezing or nudging. Legs are also used to regulate sideways (lateral) movement; as one leg encourages the horse to go sideways, the other maintains momentum and prevents the hind quarters from swinging out too far.

A rider should never kick the horse—unless in a dire emergency where the animal needs to be sent forward fast to get out of harm's way. Kicking hurts a horse. You cannot see the bruises because its coat covers them up, nor does it scream as a human would if kicked in the side, but using your legs forcefully in this way causes a horse great pain nevertheless and should be avoided.

SEAT

Bearing in mind the importance of weight in relation to the seat, in that body weight should be apportioned equally over each seat bone, the seat provides a major aid in communicating with the horse. It acts as a balancing aid to help horse and rider remain upright, helps determine the animal's power and speed, and can also act as the "brake pedal," in conjunction with hand and legs aids, when weight is lightened to ask the animal to reduce speed.

Putting more weight on one seatbone than the other acts as a signal for a horse to turn. This is more effective when also used with leg and hands aids.

VOICE

Vocal aids provide a useful back-up to other physical aids, and used in conjunction with them they help the horse understand what is required of it. The voice can be used, in appropriate pitch and tone, to praise, admonish, calm, or encourage.

When praising the horse, the voice should be enthusiastic (but not excited because this promotes tension) and used in combination with a stroke or gentle pat. "Good boy/girl" is sufficient. Clicking the tongue is another way of giving vocal encouragement. Admonishing the horse should be done immediately when necessary, with a growl—"Grrrr"—or a sharp "No!" As soon as the admonishment is done, encourage the horse again in the behavior or movement required, and praise it immediately it acquiesces so it will understand what is wanted. A horse loves to please its handler, and often a verbal ticking-off is far more effective than a physical one, since no one likes to be shouted at. Do not make a habit of shouting at your horse unnecessarily though, because this is extremely upsetting for it.

In situations where the horse requires calming down, the rider's voice is a valuable tool. Keep your voice pitched low, with the tone soothing— "Stea...dy, stea...dy, goo...d bo...y..." It doesn't matter if you talk nonsense, so long as the way of delivering the words "dampens the fire" as opposed to "fanning the flames." Talking constantly to the horse catches its attention and helps take its mind off what is worrying it, thereby helping it to relax. You'll find that this also helps you relax, which in turn reassures the horse.

Encouraging a horse to do something should be done in an enthusiastic tone. For example, when asking a horse to perform an upward transition (i.e. change the pace up a gear, such as from walk to trot), enunciate the command "trot" as "trrrrr-ot!" with the "r" being rolled and the "ot" in a quick uplifted tone. The reverse applies when asking for a downward transition (such as trot to walk). Say "walking" as "wal...king," with the last syllable enunciated in a slower downward pitch. Finally, to be absolutely sure of how to administer vocal aids, ask your instructor to demonstrate them.

HANDS

A rider's hands are used principally as guiding (steering) aids via the reins, and you must not use them to hang on to as a means of keeping your balance. At the end of those reins is the horse's mouth and great damage and pain can be caused to this by insensitive and rough handling.

Rein aids are given in conjunction with the rider's seat, weight, and leg aids. Guiding the horse is done by asking for direction via the reins, and by the amount of "yield" in the reins the hands allow. For example and in basic terms, if a rider asked the horse to turn to the right by pulling on the right rein he or she would have to allow the left rein forward slightly in order for the horse to be able to turn. At the same time if the rider did not regulate the amount of yield in the left rein and just left it slack, the horse would simply go round and round in a circle.

PERIPHERAL PHYSICAL AIDS

A person's vision, hearing, instinct, and "feel" all play important parts in riding horses competently and safely. Using your eyes and ears will help make you aware of all that is happening around you and will keep you one step ahead of the horse. If you see or hear a potential distraction or hazard, you can take steps to avoid it or keep the horse calm. For

example, a dog lurking behind a garden wall up ahead, waiting to jump up and bark; or a plastic bag blowing in the wind; or the faint sounds of an approaching large vehicle. All may alarm the horse when it actually sees them. An equine's senses of smell and hearing are much more acute than ours, but its eyesight isn't—although it fares well with long-range vision, its short-range vision is relatively poor and it is the actual seeing of a sensed hazard that prompts flight. Being aware of this, and being ready to take controlling and calming action, helps the rider contain a potentially explosive situation. Looking at the horse or the ground is a negative action that promotes negative thought. How can you expect to get from one place to another if you are not looking in the direction you want to go? If you concentrate on a point that you want to reach, you will invariably reach it.

Instinct is the natural impulse by which animals, humans included, are guided—apparently independent of reason or experience. If you feel a situation is "right" then you feel reassured; if you feel a situation is "wrong" you avoid or try to rectify it. Instinct

RIDER'S VISION

A rider's vision is a valuable natural aid because it contributes to positive thinking, so always look where you are going, in this case towards a tree, and not at your horse or at the ground.

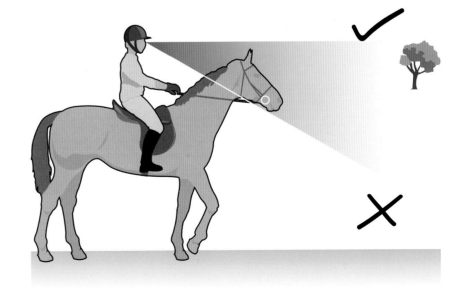

plays an important role in safe riding because a rider will not want to put himself or herself or the mount at an unacceptable risk because of self-preservation. It plays a large part in successful riding too, because if a rider senses an opportunity it encourages him or her to "go for it."

"Feel" comes with riding practice and handling horses. It describes how a person's mind and body are aware of how a horse will react in any given situation. As well as feeling physically what the horse is doing underneath you, "feel" helps promote instinctive reactions and responses in the rider toward the horse. "Feel" enables the rider to apply aids at the right moment and in the correct way, simultaneously, and at the necessary pressure and intensity. To this end, instinct and "feel" often go hand in hand.

THE HALF-HALT

A half-halt is an aid given to the horse for a variety of reasons: to attract its attention if the rider feels that its concentration is lapsing; to prepare it for a specific action, for example changing pace; to adjust the strides within a pace; to check or maintain pace; and to improve the way in which a horse carries itself within a pace, for example if the horse is becoming lazy and moving "slackly." The latter can result in a horse stumbling, so it is important it carries itself well to prevent this from happening.

A half-halt may need to be applied more than once—and repeated until it has the desired effect. It is applied via a co-ordinated sequence of aids. First the rider ensures he or she has contact with the horse's mouth via the reins. Then the rider thinks about the intended action and decides where and when to carry it out. Next, he or she simultaneously allows body

ABOVE From left to right; wrapped leather jumping whip, show cane, and dressage whip.

weight down into the saddle, uses the lower legs to nudge or squeeze the horse's sides in the girth area, and "takes" and then "gives" rein-to-mouth contact with the hands. ("Taking" consists of pulling on the reins slightly, while "giving" consists of releasing that tension without losing contact.)

USING ARTIFICIAL AIDS

WHIPS

A whip can be used as a back-up to physical aids, but it must never be used in anger to strike a horse. There are occasions when a horse ignores, or does not understand, a leg aid, and it is kinder and quicker to reinforce the aid with one smart tap behind the girth with a whip as opposed to nagging the horse's sides with the legs or resorting to kicking.

The most commonly used types of whip are the short "jumping" whip and the long schooling "dressage" whip. The dressage whip can be used without taking the hand off the reins to administer its effect (although you must take care not to interfere with the horse's mouth), while for the short whip to be applied correctly and effectively, both reins should be put in one hand and the other administers the whip.

A whip should only be employed by a proficient rider who is wise enough to know when it is required. Obviously, use of the whip can hurt a horse, especially if used incorrectly, so it is essential that a rider can judge whether its use is necessary or not.

Finally, when competing, check the competition rules regarding whips. You need to ensure whips are allowed, and you must check if there are any restrictions regarding length and type.

ABOVE A correctly fitted spur.

SPURS

Like whips, spurs should only be worn and employed by experienced riders with an independent seat who can judge when their use is necessary or beneficial to a horse. They are used to apply leg aids with more finesse, and to reinforce leg aids. They should never be used hard or roughly, for that would cause extreme pain to the horse.

As with whips, when competing, check the competition rules to ascertain if spurs are allowed, and check if there are any restrictions as to type.

MARTINGALES

Martingales are a part of the harness designed to prevent a horse from evading the bit by throwing its head up beyond a rider's point of control, and to help prevent certain undesirable actions such as rearing. The most commonly used martingales are the "running" and "standing" (see page 43).

Before a martingale is used, a horseperson should check if the horse is suffering from a physical problem that is causing its behavior. Possible reasons for this include mouth or back problems, other physiological ailments, badly fitting tack, or poor riding.

When competing, check the competition rules to see whether martingales are allowed or not.

OTHER GADGETS

Side-reins, various types of balancing rein, and "anti-evasion" bits can all have their place when necessary in the training of horses and riders, but they should always be fitted correctly and not used as a substitute for good horsemanship. As the use of such gadgets should only be employed by experienced people, they are not discussed in this book but just mentioned briefly so that you know of their existence.

When competing, check the competition rules first, to see what types of gadget, if any, are allowed.

CO-ORDINATING AIDS TO CONTROL DIRECTION AND PACE

If you have never tried the following combined actions before, try them now. First, pat your head gently and at the same time rub your stomach. Next, close your eyes and hold one arm straight out in front of you with the forefinger extended, then touch the end of your nose with that forefinger. Now sit on a chair, raise both feet off the floor, and waggle one foot up and down while simultaneously rotating the other. Then, standing up, try lifting both arms straight out from your sides, waggle one wrist up and down, and rotate the other at the same time. Now, sitting down, try the exercises together!

These are forms of brain-body co-ordination. If you find you can manage the co-ordinated actions without difficulty, great; if not, you'll find practice makes perfect. Co-ordinating your mind and body to apply aids simultaneously works in exactly the same way—and again, practice makes perfect. How aids are applied and co-ordinated to ask a horse to halt, walk on, trot, canter, and change direction are explained in the relevant chapters (Chapters Four, Six, Seven, and Eight).

LEFT Only by understanding how aids work and then mastering the techniques will you be able to communicate effectively with your horse.

On the move 3

LEFT Understanding how a horse's body is constructed and works helps a rider ride it effectively and be in harmony with it.

POINTS OF THE HORSE

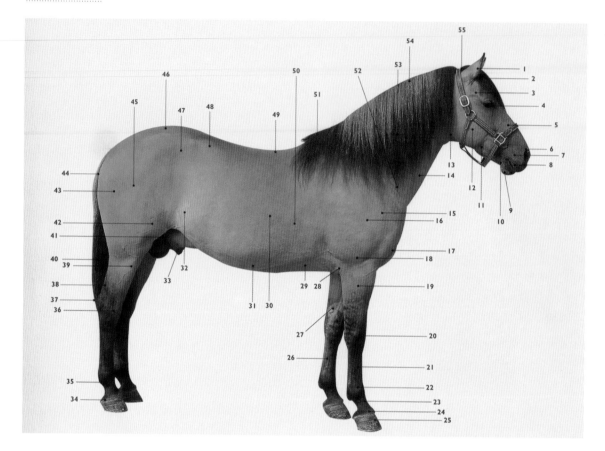

1. Ear	**20.** Knee	**39.** Gaskin or second thigh
2. Forelock	**21.** Cannon or shin	**40.** Tail
3. Temple	**22.** Fetlock joint	**41.** Stifle
4. Eye	**23.** Pastern	**42.** Thigh
5. Nose	**24.** Coronet	**43.** Buttock
6. Nostril	**25.** Hoof	**44.** Point of buttock
7. Muzzle	**26.** Splint bone	**45.** Hip joint
8. Lips	**27.** Chestnut	**46.** Croup
9. Chin	**28.** Elbow	**47.** Point of hip
10. Chin groove	**29.** Brisket	**48.** Loins
11. Branches of jaw/cheekbone	**30.** Ribs	**49.** Back
12. Cheek	**31.** Belly	**50.** Chest
13. Throat	**32.** Flanks	**51.** Withers
14. Jugular groove	**33.** Sheath	**52.** Neck
15. Point of shoulder	**34.** Heel	**53.** Mane
16. Shoulder	**35.** Ergot	**54.** Crest
17. Breast	**36.** Hock	**55.** Poll
18. Upper arm	**37.** Point of hock	
19. Forearm	**38.** Achilles tendon	

They may appear strong, and large in some cases, therefore well able to carry loads, but in fact horses were not designed to support burdens, such as people, on their backs—and most definitely not directly on the spine. For this reason it is important that any loads they do carry are balanced, distributed evenly in weight and clear of the spine, and positioned on the muscled area over the ribcage so as not to cause discomfort.

THE HORSE'S LOAD

Imagine a horse, a cob, standing 14hh (hands) and weighing 1,200lb (545kg), carrying a person of, say, approximately 132lb (60kg). The horse's load will be around 11 percent of its own bodyweight. Now imagine that 132lb (60kg) person carrying a similarly proportioned weight, which would be approximately 14lb (6.4kg). That doesn't sound like much. But put your imagination into practice and actually carry that weight around on your back for an hour or more and you will get a real indication of what a horse has to put up with.

Until they can balance properly in all paces and have achieved a secure, independent seat, novices are unstable in the saddle and ride "heavier" than their experienced counterparts who are able to adjust their balance and position with ease. To be able to derive maximum success and comfort from riding, it helps to have an idea of how they are constructed and how their bodies work. This in turn helps a rider make life more comfortable for the horse.

THE EQUINE SKELETON

The equine skeleton, simply, comprises bones, cartilage ("soft bone"), and ligaments (fibrous tissue). Cartilage supports muscles and skin, while ligaments span and connect bones together. Large bones form a framework to which large muscles are attached. This shielded "scaffolding" houses and protects the internal organs.

Young horses should not have too much work asked of them. Up to the age of five, a horse is still maturing, mentally as well as physically, and its body will not be at maximum strength. If a young horse is asked to perform strenuously at a young age, unformed bone, ligaments, and tendons may be strained, which would severely compromise the length of that animal's working life.

After the prime of life, the body's structure gradually weakens—so this should be taken into account when working elderly horses. Joints tend to be stiffer, while tendons and muscles become less elastic. Damage caused through wear and tear becomes more apparent. It takes longer for older equines to "warm up" before they can perform more active work, to avoid putting strain on stiff joints and muscles. It also takes them longer to recover after working, or following injury.

It is, however, preferable for older horses to remain in light work, as opposed to going into complete retirement, so that their bodies do not "seize up" altogether. The adage "if you don't use it, you'll lose it" applies to humans and elderly horses alike.

In order for a horse to carry a load with comfort and ease, it is essential that it is kept fit and healthy for the tasks required of it.

INTERNAL ORGANS

The kidneys are situated just under the spine where the back of the saddle rests, so the rider should take care not to sit down heavily in the saddle when mounting, nor bounce about in this area, to avoid bruising these organs.

Top (Mare)

1. Aorta

2. Left lobe of liver

3. Stomach

4. Spleen

5. Left kidney

6. Uterus

7. Esophagus

8. Trachea

9. Left vagus nerve

10. Left ventricle of heart

11. Left dorsal column

12. Small intestine

13. Left ventral colon

14. External anal
     sphincter muscle

15. Vulva

16. Urinary bladder

Bottom (Stallion)

2. Right lobe of liver

10. Right ventricle of heart

16. Rectum

17. Urinary bladder

18. Descending duodenum

19. Right kidney

20. Azygos vein

21. Right testicle

22. Body of penis

23. Lateral caecal band

24. Dorsal sac of caecum

25. Right ventral colon

26. Caudal vena cava

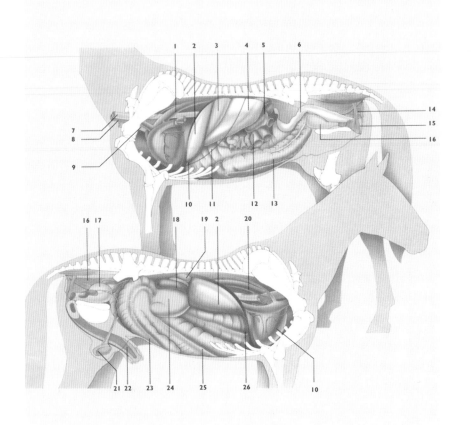

**RIGHT An example of
a trot.**

PACES OF THE HORSE

See chapters six to eight for further explanation.

WALK All four feet come into contact with the ground separately. Placed laterally, the sequence, if the horse started to walk leading with the left hind-leg, is left hind, left fore, right hind, and right fore.

TROT In a two-time gait the horse moves diagonal pairs of legs in succession, such as, right fore, left hind, and left fore, right hind. The trot is the only gait where the horse's head should be steady; if it nods, then the horse is lame.

CANTER A three-time gait, if the horse was to lead into the canter with the right foreleg, the sequence of leg movement would be left hind, right hind, and left fore simultaneously, right fore, a moment of suspension (when all four feet are off the ground), and then the left hind, etc. again.

GALLOP A four-time gait, the gallop is a fast canter. The sequence of leg movement with the left fore leading would be right hind, left hind, right fore, left fore, moment of suspension, right hind, and so on.

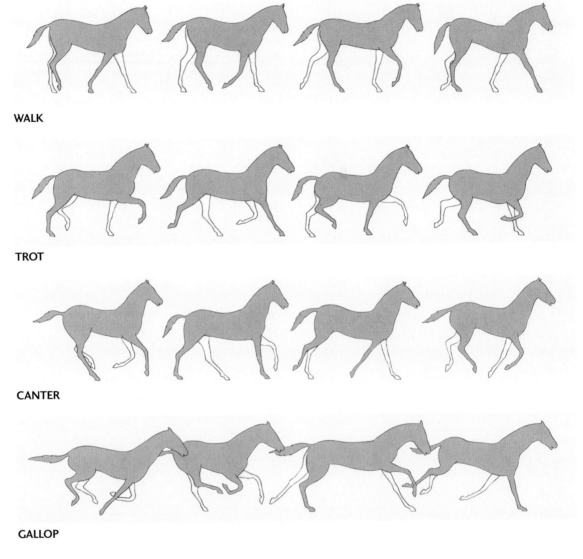

WALK

TROT

CANTER

GALLOP

EQUINE PACES

Like humans, horses tend to be stronger on one side over the other, and therefore they will favor that "better" side. Riders should strive to work horses equally on both sides, i.e. spending as much time riding in a clockwise direction as in a counterclockwise direction. Paces are best performed after a sensible warm up.

LOCOMOTION

The horse's "engine", which supplies impulsion, comprises the hindquarters and legs. These areas produce energy from behind and "push" the horse along, while the forelegs "pull."

HOW HORSES "TALK"

Equines use physical and vocal expressions to communicate their feelings and requirements. Once we humans become used to being around horses and pay attention to how they behave toward us and other horses, their expressions begin to make sense.

HOW TO UNDERSTAND WHAT A HORSE IS SAYING

Facial expressions combined with body tension and stance tell humans a lot about a horse's mood and intentions. In an aggressive mood, a horse will have its ears flat back and its face will be tense, with nostrils tight and closed, and its lips wrinkled back. Its body will be tense and ready to attack. It may also squeal, snort, or grunt loudly in anger, and its breathing may be fast and hard. In sleepy mode, the face and whole body will be "soft," with the lower lip possibly drooping, and a hind foot resting. The ears will be floppy.

If a horse is being submissive toward others, it will have a passive facial expression and look or move away. It may also "mouth" at another horse, as a foal does to its dam. Vocal communications may include whickering, snorting, squealing, and grunting.

A friendly horse will have its ears forward with a kind facial expression, i.e. it is relaxed and interested. Its body will also be relaxed.

A nervous horse, however, indicates its anxiety by flicking its ears around a lot and laying them back, rolling its eyes, and generally looking worried and tense. It will be jumpy and easily startled, and may try to avoid contact with humans or other horses. It may also pace around its stable or field, not stopping to rest.

Its respiration rate will be fast, its breathing shallow, and it may grunt or squeal sharply. A frightened horse indicates its fear by trembling, flaring its nostrils, laying its ears back, and either cowering or fleeing. It may go to the back of its stable, or a secluded corner of the field.

An excited horse will have its ears sharply forward, its eyes wide open, and it will be looking around with great interest. Its body stance will either be tense and alert, ready for action, or the animal will be prancing around as if on springs. It may also buck. Vocal accompaniment will be in the form of loud, piercing whinnies and forceful, loud, nostril-blowing and snorts.

Finally, an unwell horse may appear dejected, the head may hang low, and the ears are laid back or sideways and are floppy. The horse will be breathing either hard or shallow, with the respiration rate faster than normal, and it may be tense or trembling. Depending on the ailment, the animal may be hyperactive or may get down to roll violently. It may also sweat. Deep groaning is the usual vocal expression.

BELOW From left to right: alert and interested; sleepy, unwell, or submissive; relaxed, bored, or unwell; angry and aggressive.

FIELD OF SOUND
How the horse sees things and hears sounds has enormous bearing on its performance, and a rider must take this into account while riding. The position of the horse's ears on the sides of its head enables it to hear almost all around it. Each ear can pick up sounds to the front and side, leaving a gap immediately behind it, which it can cover with a turn of the head.

FIELD OF VISION

The shaded area in front represents the area of binocular vision, which is extremely limited. The horse's eye is one of the largest in the animal world, weighing around three ounces; the eyeball is about the size of a hen's egg.

FIELDS OF SOUND AND VISION

An unexpected appearance or sound will usually startle a horse, who may kick out or bolt as a means of self-defense, so it is important that a person approaching a horse makes his or her presence known, obviously but not loudly. For safety, approach it sideways from the front and never from directly in front or behind the horse.

A horse soon learns to associate sights with sounds. For example, at feeding time it will see its handler going into a feed-room, then hear feedbins rattling and the sound of buckets being filled. Next it will see the handler bringing the bucket of food over to it. Soon it will associate the sight of its handler going into that particular building with being fed. Sight and sound associations are important parts of equine survival—and are equally important in training a horse to obey human commands.

A horse's eye is about the size of a hen's egg and weighs about three ounces. The iris is brown, the pupil black. Some equines may have blue irises (known as "wall eyes"). Iris color has no bearing on vision quality, but blue-eyed horses can be more light-sensitive. How well horses identify colors is still uncertain. What is clear, though, is that they can determine light and dark colors as varying shades of gray.

THE HORSE'S BIT

While the bit is an important tool in communicating with and controlling a horse, great care must be taken not to abuse it. The horse's mouth is a sensitive part of the body, and its good health is essential in order that the horse can eat and drink comfortably. Rough handling of the reins will in turn act on the bit and cause great discomfort to the horse, and even injury. Imagine having a bit in your mouth with someone pulling and jabbing the reins, and you'll have an idea of what a horse can suffer.

POSTURE

Although it can do it, a horse is not ideally designed to jump. It is essential, therefore, for horse and rider to be a well-balanced partnership in order for the horse to carry out this task comfortably, effectively, and safely. The load put on the horse's front feet and legs as it lands over a jump is enormous, hence the need for a rider to be correctly positioned on landing to help minimize downforce weight.

RIDER CONFORMATION

How a rider is constructed can have a great bearing on how he or she rides. Few people are what instructors term the "perfect shape" for riding, i.e. tall and slender with weight in proportion to size, but this does not stop them from achieving riding success and enjoyment. Whatever his or her shape, it is a rider's mental attitude and technique that will decide how much or little satisfaction and success he or she will derive from the sport.

A person's shape also determines the height and type of horse he or she can ride with confidence and comfort. A tall person would probably feel unstable and "under-horsed" on a small pony, while a petite person would feel "over-horsed" and somewhat vulnerable on a big, strong, 17hh horse.

Determining your body shape will help you understand why you may have certain problems in achieving correct position and techniques. Everyone has their own particular differences. I have short legs in relation to my long trunk, which leads me to "grip up" if I'm not careful, and I also have a habit of collapsing my ribcage in an effort to alleviate pain from a hip problem, which leads to rounded shoulders. Knowing my conformation "faults" helps me to stop myself from lapsing into a poor position that affects my abilities and techniques. No rider is perfect, but you can certainly make the most of the attributes you do have, and strive to overcome any conformation problems that may hamper your riding prowess.

Whatever your shape, being fit to ride is of primary importance. Exercises that will help you tone and supple your body before, during, and after riding are discussed in Chapter Four. Becoming fit gradually is the sensible approach, ensuring you avoid stressing your body unduly. In this way, you will prevent sprains and strains —and possible painful problems later in life.

TALL WITH WEIGHT IN PROPORTION TO SIZE

Having long legs helps a rider feel more secure in the saddle because there is plenty of leg to close around the horse's sides and give leg aids with ease. Tall riders often look more elegant too. Problems tall riders sometimes encounter include being self-conscious of their size and

LEFT Different human shapes— tall with weight proportion to size; tall but thin; short with weight in proportion to size; heavy in proportion to size; short trunk with long legs; short legs with long trunk; pear-shaped.

trying to make themselves appear smaller by hunching up. Tall people can also be somewhat tense and angular in the saddle.

THIN

Being underweight can lead to a rider's body being tense and unyielding. A lack of buttock fat and muscle can make life uncomfortable in the saddle until a rider discovers how to relax and utilize his or her seat properly. A thin rider may feel self-conscious too, which saps confidence.

PETITE WITH WEIGHT IN PROPORTION TO SIZE

Small riders often try to make themselves appear taller than they are by insisting on riding big horses. However this can lead to balance and control problems. It is important for such riders to ride animals that are suited to them in terms of size and conformation. At 5'3" (155 cm) I feel most comfortable on a horse between 14hh and 15.1hh, depending on their conformation.

FAT

For safety and comfort, extremely overweight people should lose weight before taking up riding. Carrying excessive weight puts strain on the body and heart—for horse and rider alike. Those who are overweight, may find difficulty in achieving a stable and secure seat in the saddle to begin with. Other problems include an unconsciously "ham-fisted" approach, problems in recognizing and achieving feel, and a lack of

self-confidence due to their shape and weight. On the plus side, heavy riders are usually more relaxed than thin ones, and are more considerate and sensitive to the horse.

SHORT TRUNK WITH LONG LEGS

Having long legs is ideal for seat security and applying leg aids, but a short upper body generally means short arm length and reach. This can lead to a rider leaning forward in an effort to maintain contact with the horse's mouth. Hunching up is another common problem encountered, due to a lack of balance, co-ordination, and confidence.

SHORT LEGS WITH LONG TRUNK

Being "top-heavy" means a rider will often "grip up" with the knees and legs in an effort to maintain balance and seat security. However all this succeeds in doing is make the rider even more insecure. Riders with short legs have to work on toning all leg and inner thigh muscles to make their legs as long, relaxed, strong, and supple as possible in order to apply leg aids effectively and to maintain a balanced and secure seat in the saddle.

PEAR-SHAPED

Riders with large buttocks and chunky thighs find several advantages in their shape—balance and seat comfort and security being the most notable ones. However, it is important they keep their seats, thighs, and legs toned so that excess weight doesn't impede seat security and the application of effective leg aids.

RIDING—WHAT IT FEELS LIKE

For complete beginners, sitting on a horse for the first time can feel quite alien. Novices have described it in the following ways: out of control; unbalanced; unsafe; uncertain; wobbly; scary; high up; uncomfortable; but exciting and good fun nonetheless! As a horse moves, even at a slow walk, beginners may at first feel it is too fast for them to cope with. Stops, starts, and turns can be quite alarming, testing balance on a horse to the full. People have likened the feeling to sitting on a huge snake wiggling around underneath them; others have said it's similar to riding a bicycle without hands or brakes.

It is important that novices have full confidence that their instructor will control the animal at first. This helps enormously in enabling beginners to concentrate on developing their own balance and securing their body position without having to think of controlling the horse at the same time. This is why lunge lessons are so helpful at the start of a novice's riding career. (More on the subject of lungeing in Chapter Four.)

To have an idea of what balancing and sitting on a horse feels like before actually getting on one, try these simple exercises:

- **Place a length of flat wood, approximately four inches (10 cm) wide, on the ground** and then walk along it. Don't look at the ground—ensure you are looking where you are intending to go. This will help your sense of balance. This exercise gives some indication of how you can balance yourself when you are sitting on a horse.

- Sit astride a five-bar field gate with your arms and legs hanging down, relaxed. This, of course, is considerably narrower than sitting on a horse, and a lot more uncomfortable, but the height and balance factors are similar. It will accustom you to the height and balance adjustment feelings you can expect.

USING IMAGINATION AS AN AID

Imagine standing astride a narrow, fast-flowing river. The movement is tangible—you can see and feel the power of the water flowing between your legs, and watching it disorientates and unbalances you. The sheer power of that watercourse is awesome: how can you possibly hope or try to contain it? Now imagine that your seat weight, legs, and hands are dams above and on either side of that river, capable of moving down or in and out, or opening and closing in order to control the water's flow and speed. This gives some indication of how a rider's balance, position, and aids work to control a horse's motion. Putting these elements into that sort of context, riding and controlling a horse isn't that difficult after all!

Learning to ride
–the first lesson

LEFT Going for your first riding lesson can be daunting and exciting at the same time. You are taking the step forward into the wonderful world of horses where you'll learn how to look after and ride these magnificent and generous creatures, as well as make many like-minded friends.

Choosing a good riding school is paramount if you are not going to be put off at the first hurdle. For many beginners, this choice is dependent on the school's location and what it charges for lessons. However, while these are important considerations, there are other essential elements to take into account.

STEP ONE—
CHOOSING A RIDING SCHOOL

A school should be registered and licensed by the appropriate local authorities. It is preferable for it to be approved by recognized equestrian authorities too, with its instructors qualified to specified standards. In the United States, there is no federal law pertaining to licensing of riding schools, and statutory requirements vary from state to state. However, a voluntary association, the American Riding Instructors' Certification Program (ARICP) offers accreditation. Look out for license and registration or approval documents that are usually on display in the booking office of the riding school. The school should be adequately insured in case of accident or injury claims. Again, a certificate stating this will usually be displayed in a prominent position. However, if no certificates are evident, then you are within your rights to ask to see them, and it is in your interest to do so. If they fail to materialize, then think carefully before patronizing the establishment since it may not be of a reputable standard.

Finding a reputable riding school with good instructors and a varied selection of well-mannered and trained horses is paramount for the beginner. Visit several establishments and check them out before making your choice. Have a good look around to see if they appear clean, tidy, and well-run, and that the horses look contented, healthy, and well-cared for. Check to see if their stalls are clean and that their tack appears in good order and well-maintained. Dirty tack and nasty smelling, filthy stalls do not bode well.

Speak to staff and other clients at riding establishments too, so you can get a general "feel" for each place, and in order to decide whether you would be treated as a valued customer there or not. Watch some lessons in progress so you can judge if the teaching manner appeals and methods are safe and appear to work. Clients enjoying their lessons are a good sign!

LEFT Happy horses with clients and instructors enjoying lessons at a riding school are a good sign.

Once you have discovered a riding school you feel confident about, the next essential steps forward in your riding success depends on you and your instructor.

ASSESSING YOURSELF

Your future ambitions in the sport of riding will help you choose a school and instructor. If you simply want to be able to ride out safely, competently, and confidently, and maybe try your hand at a little jumping for enjoyment only, then going to a high-powered establishment or trainer may not suit you. If, on the other hand, your aims are to compete successfully in whatever discipline appeals, then going to a basic standard school may not be suitable for you.

It is essential for you, the beginner, to be brutally honest in assessing your own temperament and riding aspirations, in order that you find the school that will fulfill your expectations of the sport in the best possible way. Your temperament will only hamper your success ("contentment," as I prefer to call it) in the saddle if you let it. The biggest danger is that you allow pride and unattainable aspirations, as well as what others might think of you, to get in the way of your enjoyment of the sport at whatever level you feel comfortable. Learning to ride for your own pleasure and not for others is the biggest lesson you can ever learn when riding a horse.

If you are of a shy or timid disposition, lacking in self-confidence, then a small and friendly riding school whose instructor specializes in providing that "personal touch" is the ideal place to start your riding career. You can always progress to a more "high-powered" establishment later on if desired, when your confidence and basic riding skills have developed.

CHOOSING AN INSTRUCTOR

No matter how clean and tidy a riding school, it is the instructor who determines a rider's success in the saddle—and leaves those new to the game with lasting impressions of the sport. Good instructors have a real "feel" for their work. For a true mentor, every pupil has potential in some way, shape, or form—whether they are timid or bold, gifted or have to work hard every step of the way.

ABOVE It is important that you like, respect, and get on well with your instructor. Without a rapport between you, lessons won't be much fun and learning will be harder.

EQUINE EQUIPMENT

Being able to identify parts of the horse's tack (saddle and bridle) helps a rider grasp an instructor's commands more easily; for example, "put the reins into your outside hand and take hold of the pommel (upward curving part at the front of the saddle) with your inside hand." The girth is attached to the saddle and passes under the horse's body. Bits form part of the bridle. A neckstrap, which should always be used on riding school mounts for riders to hold onto when necessary, is a plain leather strap which is fastened around the base of the horse's neck. It should be loose enough to fit the height of two fingers under it. See Chapter Ten for instructions on fitting bridles and saddles.

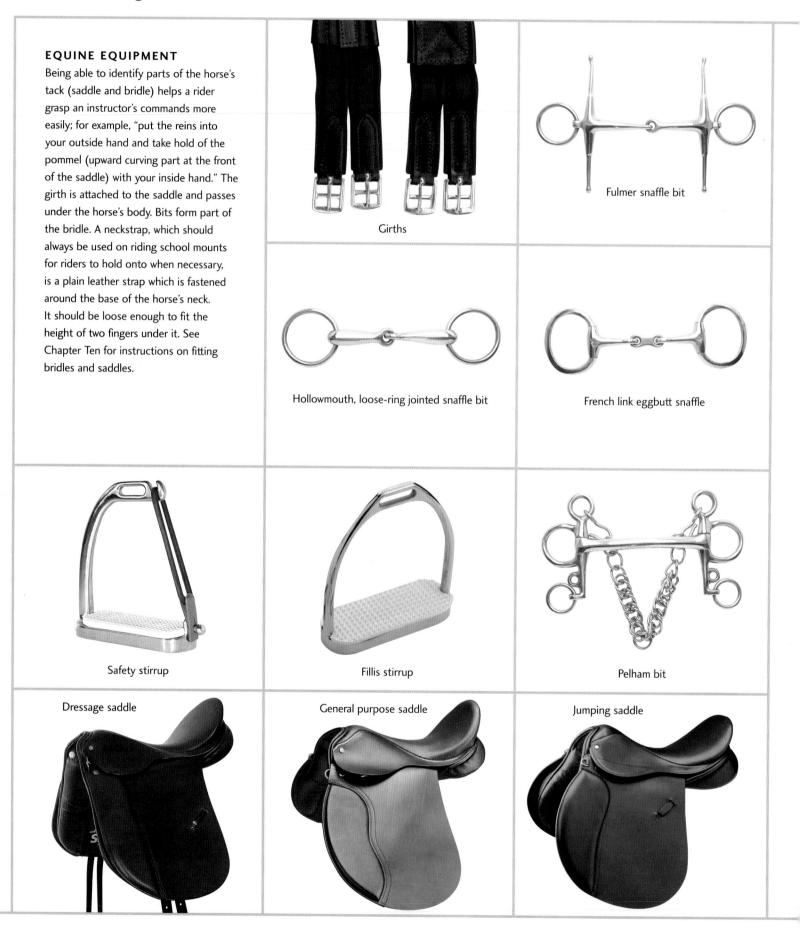

Girths

Fulmer snaffle bit

Hollowmouth, loose-ring jointed snaffle bit

French link eggbutt snaffle

Safety stirrup

Fillis stirrup

Pelham bit

Dressage saddle

General purpose saddle

Jumping saddle

An instructor should be approachable, friendly, and eager to impart knowledge. He or she should inspire respect and achievable aspiration in novice riders. Those who belittle clients' achievements cannot possibly describe themselves as "instructors," and it is important for beginners to realize that they should not put up with this treatment. It only takes a few unwisely chosen words to do immense damage to a novice rider's confidence.

Teachers, just like their clients, are all individuals and have different mannerisms, personalities, and methods of imparting their knowledge. A brisk, no-nonsense instructor is likely to strike terror into the hearts of timid novices, but will inspire more confident customers. Good teachers should be able to gauge their clients' personalities and address them accordingly.

An instructor's ability can be judged in a number of ways: by qualifications gained from a reputable equestrian organization, such as the American Riding Instructors' Certification Program (ARICP), by his or her expertise gained over years of involvement with equines, or by achievements in his or her particular discipline. An experienced rider who is talented in a particular discipline may not be gifted in imparting knowledge of riding technique.

In order to learn how to handle and ride horses well, a person must have confidence and faith in an instructor's manner and ability. A good teacher keeps things simple—both in lesson content and terminology—and goes at a pace pupils, and horses, can cope with comfortably. As well as having an affinity with clients' requirements, an instructor should take into account school horses' needs too, for without these patient and hard-working creatures there would be no riding lessons.

INDIVIDUAL VERSUS GROUP LESSONS

Ideally, beginners should start off with individual (private) lessons, as opposed to being part of a group. Once balance and security in the saddle have been achieved, as well as the basic aids of stopping, starting, and turning, then group lessons can be considered.

The advantages of group lessons are that they are less expensive and more sociable.

ON THE LUNGE

Lunge lessons enable riders to develop an independent seat and improve their balance, feel, aid co-ordination, position, and technique on a horse without the added complication of having to control it as well. The instructor keeps the horse moving at a constant and regulated pace around him or herself in a large circle, attached to a long "lunge" rein, via vocal commands that the horse is trained to respond to.

A lunge horse will be equipped with a saddle, possibly a bridle with the reins secured up so they do not dangle, a lunge cavesson (similar to a headcollar, incorporating a padded noseband with rings for the lunge rein to attach to), protective leg boots, and side reins. The latter are attached to the girth and then to the horse's bit rings or lunge cavesson. Their purpose is to

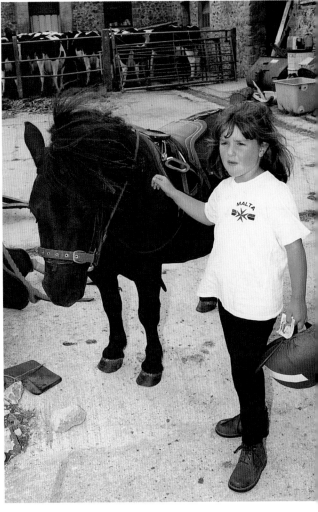

ABOVE Becoming familiar with equine equipment is an important lesson for the beginner.

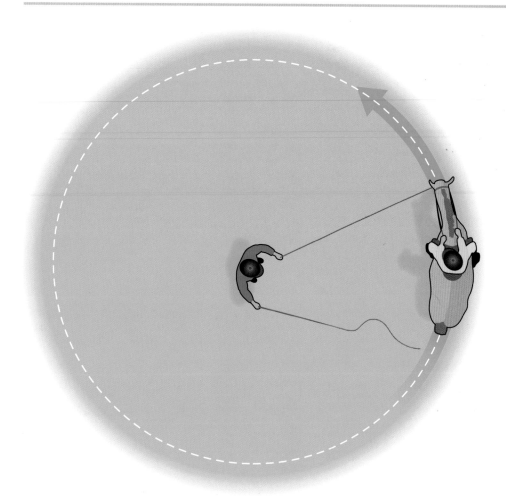

provide a "contact" and help keep the horse's head steady while it is lunged. The instructor carries a long whip, known as a lunge whip, with which he or she maintains the lunge horse's shape on the circle, and its rhythm and pace.

ABOVE An instructor moves the horse in a circle attached to a lunge rein.

STEP TWO—THE IDEAL HORSE

The success of initial riding lessons depends to a great extent on the horse you are riding. Good instructors will endeavor to match rider to horse, as to both size and temperament. Riding school horses need to be calm, quiet to handle and ride, well-mannered, and well-schooled. They also should be fit and healthy.

Nervous riders require laid-back animals; mounting such a rider on a similarly disposed horse could do irreparable damage to that person's confidence, and be unsafe. If you do not feel happy with the horse you have been given, ask if you can ride a different horse.

HANDLING AND LEADING YOUR HORSE

Initially your mount will be brought out of its stall and led into the schooling arena for you, but pay close attention to how the handler achieves this so you'll have an idea of how to do it yourself in future. Horses should be made aware that a person is coming up to them. Your movements should be calm and deliberate, not hurried or sudden. Always approach from the front, never the rear—and never walk directly behind a horse in case it kicks out. Its lead rope or reins should be held firmly with the right hand close to the head, while the left hand takes up the slack. *Do not wrap the reins or rope around your hand*, or you may be unable to let go quickly.

To lead, walk by the horse's shoulder and look where you want to go. Encourage it to walk on with your voice, and by allowing it a little slack with the right hand. To halt it, stop walking yourself and apply back pressure, as necessary, with the right hand on the lead rope or reins. When leading a horse in or out of an enclosed space, ensure the door or gate is fully open and will not blow shut on the animal as it passes through. Lead the horse straight through the opening, not at an angle, to ensure it doesn't bump itself on the door or gate posts.

Horses prefer to be stroked firmly, as opposed to patted. Do not offer tidbits by hand without first seeking permission from your instructor. Giving treats in this way encourages horses to nip people and push them around when treats are not forthcoming. Many instructors prefer to give tidbits provided by clients in the horses' feeds instead.

Drop noseband

Kineton noseband

Flash noseband

Grackle noseband

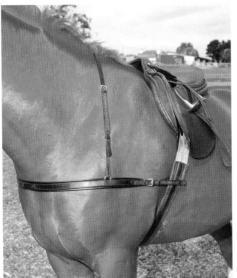

Plain cavesson noseband

Pelham bit roundings

Running martingale

Folded leather breastplate

Standing martingale

**STEP THREE—
RIDING AND SAFETY WEAR**
Investing in a body protector is sensible. These safety garments help protect vulnerable areas of the body in the event of a fall. Find an equestrian clothing retailer who is trained in fitting hats and body protectors to help you select the best possible fit and type of hat and body protector to suit your needs and shape.

Jodhpur boot

Gloves

Jodhpurs

A long rubber riding boot

Long leather riding boot

Classic helmet

Schooling helmet

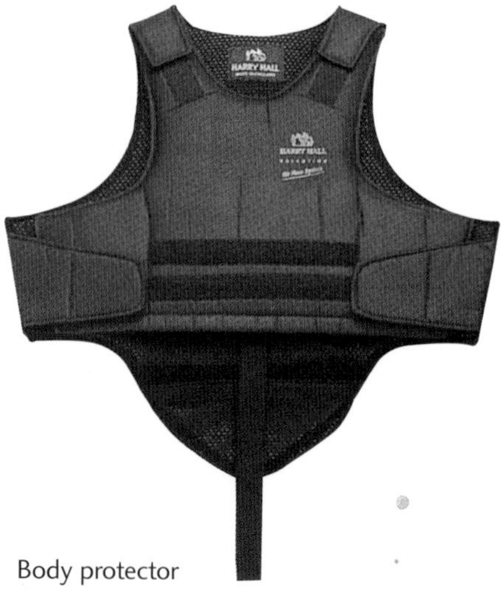

Body protector

Waterproof jacket with
fleece lining

Fleece jacket

Cotton top

RIDING WEAR

Essential items for novice riders are a helmet, boots, and gloves. Dark-colored jodhpurs are more practical to begin with for casual riding than white or cream, and are more flattering for the fuller figure. The choice is vast, with prices ranging from budget to expensive depending on what you want and can afford. Always purchase a helmet with a three-point harness and one that conforms to current safety standards (American standard ASTM F1163). For casual riders, a schooling helmet with a cover (which is called a "silk") is the generally the most popular choice. They need less cleaning than velvet helmets and you can use a velvet silk for future competitions when appropriate. You will only need riding jackets (tweed or black/navy blue) for competition. Never buy second-hand hats because they may have had a bump at some time, causing their protective qualities to be reduced, but other items can be purchased second-hand if your budget is limited.

Hacking jackets

ABOVE Mounting a horse correctly.

BOTTOM RIGHT Dismounting a horse correctly.

TOP RIGHT Getting a leg up.

STEP FOUR—MOUNTING, DISMOUNTING, AND RIDING POSITION

MOUNTING A HORSE

Mounting is usually carried out on the left-hand side of the horse, but it is useful to perfect mounting from both sides.

- Ensure that the girth is secured and tight (you should still be able to slide the flat of your hand between it and the horse), and that the saddle is correctly placed on the horse's back.
- Check that the stirrup leathers are approximately the right length. Do this by letting the stirrups down, then by closing your fist and putting it up to the stirrup bar (where the stirrup leather joins the saddle), then stretch the leather and stirrup iron out under that arm toward your armpit. The iron should fit snugly up against your armpit.
- Stand at the horse's shoulder, facing its rear.

- Gather the reins (and whip if carried) up to take contact with the horse's mouth and put them in your left hand, before placing it in front of or on the pommel.
- Half-turn the stirrup iron clockwise toward you with your right hand, then place your left foot in the iron.
- Hop around close to the horse and place your right hand over the waist (center) of the saddle, holding the offside skirt at the top of the saddle for security.
- Then spring up off your right foot, leaning forward slightly and lift your right leg up

and over the horse's back, taking care not to kick it.

- Sit down gently in the saddle and place your right foot in its stirrup iron.
- Lightly take up rein contact with both hands.

Ideally, when mounting, there should be someone holding the opposite stirrup down and steady to help prevent the saddle slipping across the horse's back.

Having the use of a mounting block is a boon for horse and rider alike—it makes mounting so easy. A major advantage to this mounting method is that it limits strain on the horse's back and saddle tree.

DISMOUNTING A HORSE

Dismounting is usually done on the left-hand side of the horse, but practice on both sides.

- Ensure that the horse is standing still.
- Take your feet out of the stirrup irons.
- Put the reins (and whip if carried) into your left hand and rest it on the horse's neck.
- Put your right hand on the pommel.

- Simultaneously lean forward slightly, and swing your right leg back and over the horse's quarter, being careful not to kick it.
- Allow yourself to slide down and off the horse, landing gently and facing forwards.
- Keep hold of the horse.

GETTING A LEG-UP

Having a leg-up onto a horse is another method of mounting, and again one that limits strain on the horse's back and saddle tree. Remember to sit down gently in the saddle, rather than "thump."

RIGHT The correct riding seat, seen from the back, the side, and from the front.

RIDING POSITION

FOOT PERFECT

Stirrup iron size and the position of the foot are very important. The pictures below show from left to right, a stirrup that is too small, too big, and correct.

STEP FIVE—MOVING ON THE LUNGE REIN

Now the fun starts! Because of all the preparation involved, it often seems as though you will never actually get to move anywhere on a horse, but this procedure is essential to your safety and so that you are clear and confident about what to expect and what you should do.

Now that you are actually on a horse, you will experience a multitude of feelings and sensations. First, you will feel incredibly high up off the ground and, second, you will feel rather helpless, because you don't know how to start or stop the animal you are sitting on. You'll experience elation and fear at the same time, your body and limbs may feel stretched, strained, and uncomfortable, being in positions that are alien to them.

For a beginner, even the smallest movement requires much physical effort and balance adjustment. Novice riders often try too hard, which in turn makes them tense, therefore hampering progress. The key rule once you are on a horse is to relax, listen to what your instructor is telling you, and endeavor to do as directed. Initial lunge lessons will consist of walk only, so you can get used to sitting on a moving horse. Learning how to balance on and move with the horse, not against it, is the main aim at this point.

Holding the reins does not usually happen until you have achieved an independent and stable seat. This is to prevent the rider from using the reins as a balancing aid, which would cause the horse's mouth to be pulled and jabbed. Instead, the rider will hold the pommel or a neckstrap at first, to help maintain balance. Looking where you are going will also help you balance.

STEP SIX—MOUNTED EXERCISES

ABOVE AND RIGHT
Mounted exercises on the lunge help tone and supple the rider's body, improve balance and coordination, and promote confidence.

STEP SEVEN—QUESTION TIME

Q: *Is it normal for my legs and bottom to hurt so much after a lesson, and can I avoid this happening in the future?*
A: Because riding involves muscles you don't normally use, you are bound to feel a little sore after a lesson. Soreness is usually most intense the following day. However, the more warming-up exercises you do before mounting and when in the saddle, the less sore you should be. Staying relaxed in the saddle also helps alleviate stress on muscles.

If you are hurting during a lesson (and that goes for having a "stitch" too), tell your instructor immediately so he or she can slow things down or stop, so that you don't continue to put pressure on sore areas.

If you are still sore from a previous lesson, ask your instructor if you can be provided with a "seat-saver"—a soft, cushioned pad that is placed on top of the saddle.

Q: *How soon will I be allowed off the lunge?*
A: This depends on your ability to balance, and your confidence. Until your instructor and you both feel you can control the horse on your own, off the lunge, it is better to remain on it.

Q: *What is the difference between a horse and a pony?*
A: For the purposes of making things simple, horses and ponies are all referred to as "horses" in this book. Horses and ponies are generally determined by height: a pony measures 14.2hh and under; a horse measures over 14.2hh. A hand measures four inches (10 cm).

Q: *I seem to struggle to maintain my position in the saddle. Is there an exercise I can practice at home to help me solve this problem?*

A: There certainly is and it will enable you to gain an understanding of what constitutes a good riding position without getting on a horse. Use a mirror to check your posture, as the sensation of being upright can be misleading.

- Stand upright and place your feet about two feet (60 cm) apart, ensuring they are level with each other and that equal weight is placed on them.
- Keeping your body upright, bend your knees a little and incline your head forward slightly until you just see your toes in front of your kneecaps.
- Then, maintaining that body position and allowing weight to travel down squarely into your feet, raise your head up again.
- That's as close as you can get to the riding position on a horse.

TAKING STOCK

After your lesson has ended, you may find that you experience a variety of emotions and feelings—euphoria, relief, bewilderment, pride, and also worry that you may not have done as well as you had hoped or as your instructor expected. Your legs and seat will possibly feel a little sore too. With luck, though, your overriding feeling will be one of impatience for the next lesson.

It is usually only when you get home that you suddenly think of all the things you wanted to ask your instructor but forgot. You will then also have time to analyze your lesson. Perhaps the lesson was not as you expected. Common first-lesson problems encountered include:

- **Finding the instructor daunting—maybe he or she was too overbearing, loud, impatient, or didn't explain instructions clearly and simply.**
- **The horse was not right—it was too big, small, disobedient, uncomfortable, or bad-tempered.**
- **The saddle was uncomfortable.**
- **Feeling unsafe and anxious due to an unsuitable horse or instructor.**

Sadly, some people are put off riding due to bad first-time experiences and not knowing how to cope with them.

TAKING CHARGE OF YOUR OWN DESTINY

You, as the client, must find the courage to tell your teacher if there is anything worrying you, or if you do not understand any instructions and require further explanation.

If you find your instructor abrupt or impatient, you will feel anxious and rushed, and this is neither safe nor conducive to learning. You must voice your concerns to your instructor in order that they can be addressed to your satisfaction. If this fails, find a different riding school.

For enthusiastic beginners, having to take things slowly at first can be frustrating, and this in itself can hamper progress. You must channel that frustration into positive thinking and aim to complete each task you are presented with positively and enthusiastically, in order to progress at the pace you want.

School exercises 5

LEFT The schoolroom: An open-air enclosure used for teaching riding is known as an outdoor arena, outdoor school, or manège. Under cover, they are known as indoor schools or arenas.

Beginner riders are generally taught the basics in an enclosed schooling area, which usually measures 40 m x 20 m (120 x 60 feet). Specific letters of the alphabet are often used to mark certain points around the arena.

A SENSE OF SECURITY

Being in an enclosed area will enable you to feel secure in the knowledge that the horse cannot go very far and that the instructor is close enough to lend a hand and take control of a situation when necessary. You are close enough, as is the horse, to the instructor to see and hear commands clearly. You are given instructions to reach certain points, marked by letters, of the arena, which again instills positive thinking and a feeling of security. The principal school letters are A K E H C M B F, which are easy to learn as "All King Edward's Horses Can Manage Big Fences." These are positioned as right.

WHAT ARE THE LETTERS FOR?

The letters mark out the school at set distances and are there for several reasons. They are used to identify certain points around the arena so that a rider has points to aim for. They enable an instructor to identify points where he or she requires school movements or changes of pace to be done. The "letter system" as this is known is a fundamental part of dressage and classical horsemanship in North America and is the ideal in establishing a firm foundation in this discipline.

RIGHT A 40 x 20-meter (120 x 60-foot) manège layout.

BELOW A 60 x 20-meter (180 x 60-foot) manège layout.

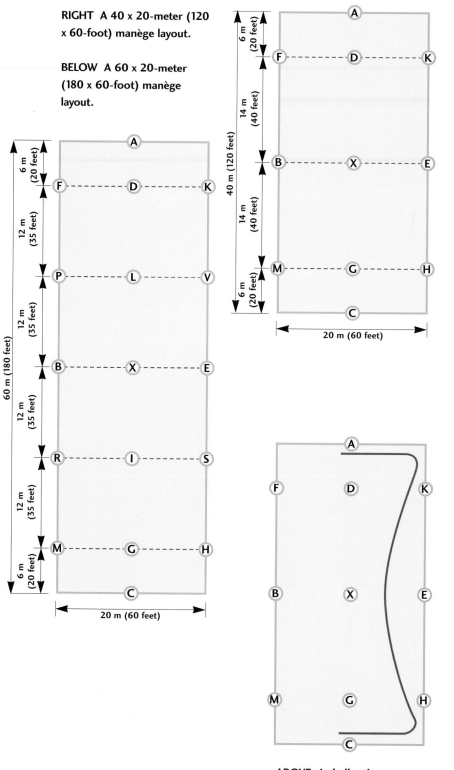

ABOVE A shallow loop.

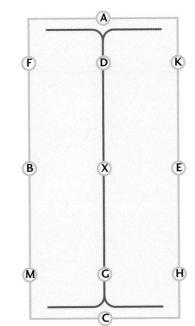

ABOVE Riding around the inside track and the outside track of the manège, the latter known as "going large."

ABOVE Center (long) line changes of rein.

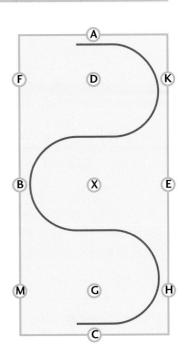

ABOVE Middle (short) line changes of rein.

ABOVE Three loop serpentine from A-C, C-A.

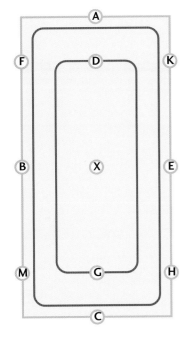

ABOVE Changing rein on diagonal from M-K, F-H

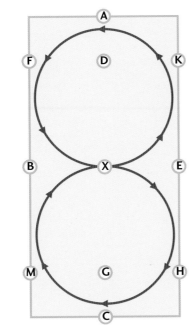

ABOVE Changing the rein out of a 20 meter (60 foot) circle onto another 20 meter (60 foot) circle.

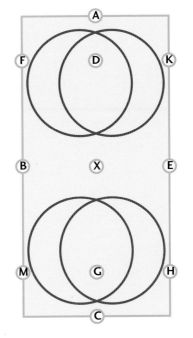

ABOVE 15 meter (50 foot) circles.

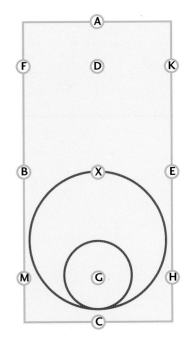

ABOVE 10 meter (30 foot) circle from 20 meter (60 foot) circle.

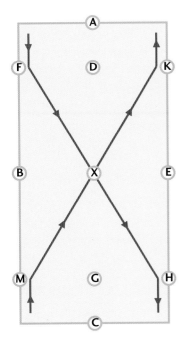

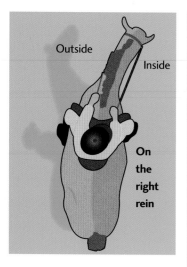

Outside

Inside

On the right rein

KNOWING "INSIDE" FROM "OUTSIDE"

A rider and horse's "inside" is the one nearest the center of the school, while the "outside" is the one nearest the sides of the building.

WHAT IS THE PURPOSE OF SCHOOL EXERCISES?

Riding straight lines, loops, turns, and circles, and changing pace at letters, helps a rider learn how to co-ordinate aids and techniques in order to direct a horse as required. Exercises are given particular names, for example a 20 meter (66 foot) circle or a serpentine, so that a direction is clearly understood by the rider.

TRACKS

The path around the sides of the school is known as the "outside track;" the path within the outside track is known as the "inside track" (see page 53).

CHANGING THE REIN

This means simply changing the direction from clockwise to counterclockwise or vice versa. How you do this depends on the method requested; for example, on the left rein (counterclockwise), "change the rein across the diagonal from H to F."

FREE LESSONS

One of the best ways to pick up hints and tips is to watch other people having riding lessons—both novice and experienced riders. It's an invaluable method of increasing your theoretical knowledge of equestrian. You'll soon learn what the terms used mean and how to go about executing them.

FILM STARS

While school mirrors are useful in helping you keep an eye on your position, having someone video your progress is extremely beneficial. You can see where you are going wrong, and how to correct it.

Riding off the lunge – learning to walk 6

LEFT A rider's first lesson off the lunge will be both exciting and slightly daunting. Putting into practice all you learned on the lunge—balance and aids—while controlling the horse at the same time isn't quite as easy as experienced riders make it appear. Remember, though, that everything will fall into place sooner or later.

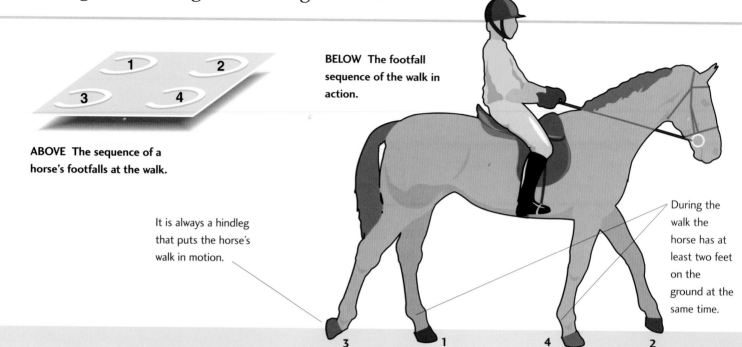

ABOVE The sequence of a horse's footfalls at the walk.

BELOW The footfall sequence of the walk in action.

It is always a hindleg that puts the horse's walk in motion.

During the walk the horse has at least two feet on the ground at the same time.

Like setting off on an adventure, the experience of being allowed off the lunge for the first time is for many one full of promise combined with a feeling of apprehension. Part of you cannot wait to put all the techniques you learned on the lunge into practice, thinking "I can do this!," but the other part wonders "what if my horse won't obey my directions?" This is where employing the power of positive thinking plays an important role: Remember, there's no such word as "can't." You can feel secure in the knowledge that the horse cannot go very far because it is in an enclosed arena, and your instructor is on hand to assist, encourage, and guide you every step of the way.

Before he or she "goes it alone", a rider must bear in mind the following possible reasons as to why a horse does not respond to the aids and directions as desired and expected. Understanding these reasons is essential to good, sympathetic riding:

- **The aids have been given ineffectively or incorrectly.**
- **The horse does not understand the aids given.**
- **The horse cannot physically do what has been asked of it. This could be due to it being unfit for the work, feeling unwell, or being in pain from an ailment, from badly fitting tack, or from a rider sitting poorly and presenting a burden for the horse.**
- **The horse is disobeying your commands.**

It takes time and experience to be able to recognize why a horse is not "listening" to you, so until you have gained this knowledge do not reach for the whip first and your brain second! Getting angry or frustrated with the horse—or with yourself for that matter—will do no good at all and more than likely will exacerbate an awkward situation and hamper your progress. Your instructor will help you gauge your actions by advising you why a horse is behaving in a certain way. Progress is more sure to come slowly but surely; it is essential to understand

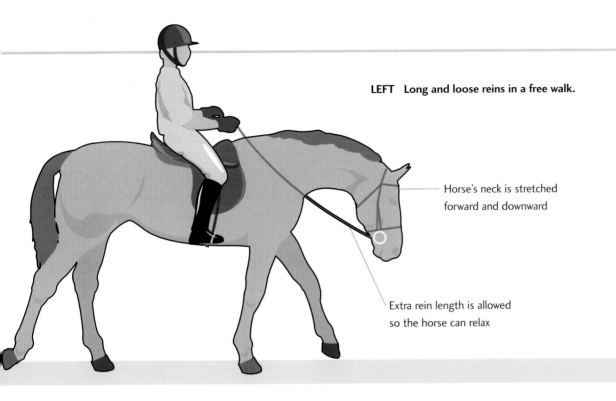

LEFT   Long and loose reins in a free walk.

Horse's neck is stretched
forward and downward

Extra rein length is allowed
so the horse can relax

IN THE SEAT

The saddle plays an important part in the rider achieving a comfortable and effective position on a horse. Some riders struggle endlessly to maintain a good leg and seat position, without realizing that no matter how hard they try, the saddle is in fact working against them because the stuffing is unlevel, the seat is badly designed, the flaps are not the right size and shape, the tree is twisted, or the stirrup bars are not positioned ideally. This saddle (below) slopes back from pommel (upward curve at the front) to cantle (raised curve at the back) and the stirrup bars are too far forward, so the rider will keep slipping to the back of the saddle and will find it hard to maintain the desired shoulder-hip-heel line. Here the rider's leg is positioned too far back.

each stage of learning to ride, and be able to put it into practice, before moving to the next.

HOW THE HORSE MOVES AT THE WALK

The walk is a four-time gait (pattern of leg movements), meaning that the horse places each foot down on the ground individually. It has at least two feet on the ground at the same time. Although you might think that a front leg would begin setting the horse in motion, it is in fact a hindleg that starts it (to "push" the horse along). An active (or "medium") yet calm walk is determined by the horse "tracking up" (or "overtracking"). Tracking up describes when the horse's hindfeet touch the ground in front of the hoofprints made by the forefeet. This indicates the horse is alert and energetic (and therefore likely to respond to aids quickly) and has enough forward movement to propel itself along properly. A lazy, sluggish walk can cause all sorts of problems; the horse isn't alert or energetic enough to listen to or respond to its

rider's aids; it hasn't enough impulsion to perform the pace in balance properly; it tends to put its weight on its forehand (the part of the horse in front of the saddle) and lean on the rider's hands, making it heavy and awkward to ride; and the horse runs the risk of stumbling.

THE FREE WALK

The free walk, or "walking on a long rein," describes when the rider allows rein length so that the horse can relax. It does this by stretching its neck forward and downward, but contact should not be lost. The free walk is allowed as and when it is appropriate, e.g. after a period of work or to reward the horse for something well done. Giving a "loose rein" means just that, and is done at the end of a working session to allow the horse to stretch fully and "chill out."

The two other types of walk—collected and extended—require more advanced knowledge and technique to achieve, and are therefore not included in this book, which simply deals with the basics of riding competently and safely.

ABOVE If the rider is too stiff or too relaxed, he or she will tip forward as the horse halts, and tip back as it goes forward into the walk.

THE RIDER'S POSITION ON THE HORSE

As discussed in Chapter Two, it is important that the rider sits in the right position in relation to the horse's center of gravity (wherever that may be depending on the movement) in order to help both horse and rider balance. You will have learned on the lunge where the equine center of balance is and where to sit in relation to it. An effective riding position and posture is essential to being able to maintain balance in all paces and movements, and in applying aids effectively. That effective position is:

- Sitting up tall, yet relaxed ("soft"), in the deepest part of the saddle's seat, with equal weight on both seatbones. There should be a slight hollow at the base of the back. No hollow means the rider is inclined to slouch with the chin jutting out, while a deep hollow means the rider is too stiff and perching uncomfortably on his or her seat, specifically the fork (pubic bone). To check the depth of the back hollow, place both reins into one hand and fold the other arm across the base of your back. Adjust your position so there is a slight indentation in your back.

- Ideally, shoulders should be level, relaxed, and maintained squarely over the hips. Dipping one shoulder invariably means the rider is collapsing one hip, rendering those parts of his or her body immobile and unable to contribute to movement.

- Elbows should be bent, with the joints relaxed, close in to the rider's sides. There should be a straight line from elbows to hands, continuing down along the reins to the horse's mouth. Hands should be level with each other and held on either side of the horse's neck, approximately three inches (8 cm) above the withers. Thumbs lie flat over the forefingers and the closed fists face each other.

Riding off the lunge—learning to walk

- The stirrups should be neither too long nor too short. Hanging loose, the stirrup iron should lie level with the rider's ankle bone. They can be later lengthened as required.
- The rider should be looking ahead, with the neck against the back of the collar. The chin should not be tucked in too much, otherwise a stiff and unnatural upper position will result, nor should it jut out, or slouching will occur.
- Knees should be bent, soft, and "open," as opposed to straight, tense, and closed tight into the saddle flap.
- The lower legs should be against the horse's sides just behind the girth area, ready to apply aids as necessary.
- Stirrup irons should be placed on the widest part of the foot's sole, with the toes forward or out slightly (whichever is most comfortable for the rider) and the heels allowed to drop down (never forced down).
- Sitting correctly on a horse, a straight line should be drawn from a rider's ear down through the shoulder, hip and ankle bone. Use school mirrors, if available, to check your position.

Sometimes it may be necessary to adopt a different, or alternative, position to help a horse maintain balance or to try out different techniques as appropriate.

MAINTAINING POSITION

Whatever pace you are engaged in, your aim should be to maintain your position with the minimum of effort and tension. Working hard to remain in balance results in stiffness, tiredness, and being totally ineffective on the horse. To help you avoid becoming stiff and tense, try any or all of the following exercises while mounted: rotate your shoulders; circle arms one at a time; tip your head from side to side; rotate your wrists and ankles (take your feet out of the stirrup irons first); swing your legs backward and forward; and stretch up and then relax.

ABOVE The rider's knee should be relaxed and open: This allows upper body weight to travel down into the legs and heels; enables the legs to operate effectively; and helps maintain the rider's position, suppleness, and balance.

BELOW Changing the whip from one hand to another.

RIGHT From left to right: reins held too loosely; correct position; hands facing down; crossing the hands.

HOLDING THE REINS

Developing a feel for contact—knowing how much "give" and "take" to allow on the reins—comes with experience. It is important though, to keep your fingers closed firmly on the reins so that they do not slip through them unintentionally or when the horse pulls against your hands or tosses its head.

AIDS FOR THE WALK

BELOW Holding a whip incorrectly, and bottom, correctly.

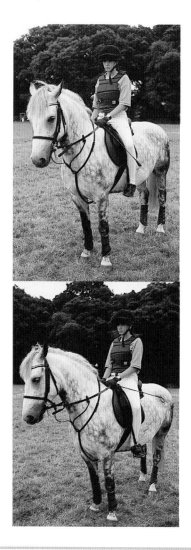

- Check that the horse is listening to you (i.e. ready, willing, and able) by applying a half-halt, or as many as necessary, as described on page 24.
- Next, close (squeeze) your legs onto the horse's sides, allow weight into the saddle, and, as you feel the horse begin to move, allow your rein contact to give so that the horse can stretch its neck out as needed to achieve forward momentum.
- Allow your hands to travel with the horse's head and neck movement in walk. If they are too rigid, then rein contact will be intermittent, loose one minute and jabbing the horse in its mouth the next; if they are too loose, then you will have no contact to guide with at all.
- Allow your body to move with the horse rather than sit tensely and be jolted about. You should feel each seatbone moving forward in time to the horse's pace and motion of its back muscles. Be aware of not allowing your body to tip back as the horse moves from halt to walk, and tipping forward as it slows from walk to halt.
- Your aim is to maintain a regular rhythm at the same pace, not allowing the horse to slow down and dawdle or stop, nor walk faster and faster. Maintain this rhythm with your seat, weight, legs, hands, and half-halts when needed.
- Keep your legs close to the horse's sides so they are ready to apply aids, but do not constantly squeeze and "nag" with them, as the horse will become "dead to the leg" and take no notice of them.
- Remember always to look where you are going! Use your power of positive thinking to enable your body to carry out what you require of it, and also to help your body respond to the horse as necessary.
- To maintain a straight line, keep your

weight equally distributed in the saddle, your rein contact equal in both hands and leg contact equal. If you feel the horse deviating from that line, you need to steer it back on course by using your seat, legs, and hands appropriately. For example, if the horse is veering to the left, guide it back over to the right by closing your left leg on the girth area as firmly as necessary to "push" it over, support with your right leg to prevent the horse overcorrecting and veering right, maintain equal seat weight, and take up a little more contact with your right hand. Once back on the straight line,

RIGHT As the horse walks, its head will nod up and down slightly. The rider's hands must follow this movement, forward and backward slightly, to allow the horse freedom to move, to avoid jabbing the horse in the mouth, and to maintain contact with its mouth.

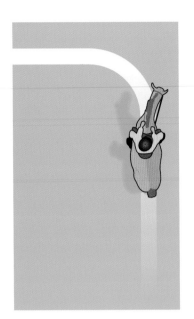

ABOVE The top illustration shows the incorrect bend for negotiating a left hand corner and below is the correct bend.

equal up your position again. It's similar to steering a yacht in the wind or driving a car; you need to keep making small adjustments in order to stay on course.

• Maintain impulsion by using your legs and seat. Losing impulsion leads to the horse leaning on its forehand and therefore on your hands, making it heavy and unyielding to ride, as well as at risk from stumbling.

AIDS FOR HALT

• Ensure the walk is steady, rhythmical, and has sufficient impulsion. A dawdling walk won't result in a decent transition (change of pace) when and where you want it to happen, and neither will a fast, erratic walk.

• Half-halt to gain the horse's attention and to alert him that you are about to ask him to carry out a task.

• Simultaneously lighten your weight in the saddle, close your legs on the girth area gently, both to maintain impulsion into the halt and to keep him standing square, and keep your hands from moving (do not pull back on the reins!) with its forward motion. The horse effectively walks into a "dead end."

• Once halted, maintain the horse's state of alertness and readiness for action by remaining alert yourself while sitting quietly. Do not "go to sleep" in halt because you need to be ready to take action should the horse be spooked or move off unbidden.

AIDS FOR TURNING

• Sit square in the saddle with weight equally distributed over both seatbones. Ensure you keep your hips parallel to the horse's.

It's tempting to lean in the direction you want to go, and as a result collapse one side of your body, but it is important that you resist this because not only will it encourage the horse to "motorbike" around a turn, it will also hamper your ability to use your body properly and apply aids effectively.

• Ask the horse to look in the direction you want to go by increasing contact on the appropriate rein, while giving slightly with the other hand. When flexing its neck properly in the direction of a turn, you should be able to see the corner of the horse's inside eye.

• Close the inside leg on the girth. This acts as a "support" for the horse to "bend" around and asks the horse to move away from that leg. The outside leg is employed behind the girth to maintain impulsion and prevent the horse's quarters from swinging out too far on the turn.

• While the inside hand, asks for bend, the outside hand regulates the amount of bend to the inside and also helps control the pace.

Getting the idea of co-ordinating aids simultaneously may take you quite a long time, but never lose sight of the fact that sooner or later it will all click into place and feel natural. When you don't succeed just keep trying. In a nutshell, whatever the pace, this is how leg and hand aids work:

• The inside leg creates and maintains impulsion. It also asks for bend and lateral (sideways) movement.

• The inside hand asks for bend.

• The outside leg controls the amount of bend requested by the inside leg and hand

by controlling the horse's quarters. It also maintains impulsion.

- The outside hand helps control bend, speed, and impulsion.

WORKING WITHOUT STIRRUPS

When taught and done properly, riding without stirrups is a great way of helping a rider establish balance, achieve a deeper, secure, and independent seat, and be able to feel the horse's movement more intensely. For these reasons, it can be extremely beneficial in instilling confidence in a rider. Initially it should be taught on the lunge so that the rider does not have to worry about controlling the horse. Off the lunge, it is most beneficial when done for short amounts of time only (it is tiring and will cause discomfort to both horse and rider if overdone). To help a rider feel more secure in the saddle without stirrups, reins should be put in the outside hand while fingers on the inside hand hook under the pommel for security and to "pull" the rider down into the saddle until he or she achieves stability. Working without stirrups helps achieve a longer, more relaxed and stable leg position. It also helps the rider feel his or her seatbones, and learn to apportion weight equally on them.

However, if done incorrectly or inappropriately, working without stirrups can encourage riders to "grip up" with their knees, therefore negating the object of the exercise. A comfortable horse and saddle is essential for this exercise. If the saddle flaps are not the right length then they may interfere with the tops of the rider's boots. A deep-seated dressage-style saddle is preferable, as is a horse with rhythmic, comfortable paces and a steady head carriage. If necessary, to enhance rider comfort, a seat-

saver should be used. An uncomfortable rider will not gain any benefit from the exercise. If it is carried on for too long, the rider will become tired and sore. Five minutes on each rein is plenty initially. It is important that confidence, and control in the walk are achieved before attempting the trot and the canter.

CROSSING OVER STIRRUPS

This is done in preparation for working without stirrups, so that they do not hamper horse or rider. Ideally the stirrups should be removed, but this is often impractical due to the time involved in removing then attaching them again.

- Ensure your horse is standing still and calm.
- Take your feet out of the stirrups.
- Pull the tops of the leathers up and free of the stirrup bar.
- Fold the right stirrup over the horse's neck, in front of the saddle first, ensuring that the buckle lies flat. Repeat with the left.
- Ensure that the irons do not become trapped between the saddle and the horse.
- To take stirrups back, simply uncross them with the left first. Do not let them fall down, because they may bump painfully against the horse's elbow or startle it. Pull down on the bottom leathers to slide the buckle back up to the stirrup bar, then replace your feet in the irons.

ABOVE Riding without stirrups.

If you fall off, simply take down the left stirrup and remount, then cross that stirrup over again.

NERVES

Being scared of something when you ride is nothing to be ashamed of. Fear is a powerful tool and, like any instrument, must be used correctly if you are to obtain its benefit. Employed in a positive way it is a valuable safety device, helping prevent you from putting yourself and your horse at an unnecessary risk. Used in a negative way, it can hamper your learning potential both mentally and physically.

You, as the client, have the ultimate power to refuse to do something that you do not want to do. If you choose to exercise that right, then do so positively. Study the experience, the reasons for your fear and how you can overcome it, and use what you learn to build solid blocks on which to progress, not regress. If taught properly, a rider should not feel real "gut-churning" fear at any time—merely apprehension at doing something new. That in itself is an important lesson.

QUESTION TIME

Q: *How fast does a horse move in the walk?*
A: It depends on the size of the animal and the length of its strides, so between three miles (5 km) an hour up to five or six (8 or 10 km).

Q: *I am really scared about hurting myself if I fall off. Is there any way I can minimize damage?*
A: An important factor in lessening the risk of injury is to relax. A tense body is more prone to damage because it does not absorb shock well. Try to curl into a ball and protect your head. Do not throw an arm out to save yourself as that arm will bear the brunt of the fall.

Q: *Although my instructor is patient and does his or her best to explain things. I cannot seem to grasp what I should be doing.*
A: Riding is best taught by an instructor explaining what is required, why and how to achieve it, and then giving a demonstration of how a certain movement should be done properly. Finally, the instructor should encourage the client to try it out. If you still don't understand, ask the instructor to demonstrate.

TAKING STOCK

Learning to walk, halt, and turn are the basic essentials in riding. For any enthusiastic beginner, being unable to progress to the trot and the canter until you have mastered these basics can be frustrating. But taking things step by step, and this can be slow or fast depending on your ability, is essential to the welfare and well-being of both rider and horse. Being able to maintain a constant walk rhythm on a horse, being able to turn it, and being able to halt it are all major achievements to aim for.

SELF-HELP

- Beneficial exercises include cycling, swimming, walking, and jogging. Mucking-out stables and grooming horses is also a great way to keep fit.
- Read as many horsy books as you can to expand your equestrian knowledge.
- A good rider needs to practice patience, self-discipline, positive thinking, sensitivity, and thoughtfulness. He or she must also never be afraid to question the instructor if something is not understood.

Learning to trot 7

LEFT There are few things more thrilling than the first sensation of sitting on a trotting horse.

ABOVE The trot sequence of footfalls in action.

BELOW The sequence of a horse's footfalls at the trot.

A basic, and good, working trot should be active and freely performed with a regular rhythm and constant pace. It should also feel balanced, with a "swing" to it that denotes that the horse is happy, relaxed, and has sufficient impulsion. A lazy trot feels heavy, wooden, and "lumpy." Some horses are naturally bouncier than others, which can make life difficult for a beginner, so it is preferable that a novice learns on a steady and comfortable horse.

HOW THE HORSE MOVES AT THE TROT

The trot is a two-time movement, meaning that the horse's legs move in diagonal pairs —left hind with right fore, right hind with left fore. There is a moment of suspension when all four feet are off the ground at the same time.

As it trots, the horse's head should be still; if the horse "nods", then it means that it is suffering a physical problem or has become lame. Because the head is still, so should the rider's hands be, remaining relaxed and yielding as necessary. If the rider's hands bounce, then this indicates tension in the body. Imagine you are carrying a glass of water in each hand and you do not want to spill that water. Allow your body to absorb the horse's movement

underneath you—it is impossible to keep your hands still until you have developed a stable seat.

TYPES OF TROT

Beginners will work in the "working" trot, otherwise referred to as the "active" trot. Other types of trot are "medium," "collected," and "extended," but these are more advanced forms of the trot movement so are not discussed here.

THE RIDER'S POSITION

This is exactly the same as for the walk (see page 58) and the same principles apply. However, in the posting trot you need to incline forward slightly from the hips as you rise in order to avoid getting left behind the horse's movement.

HOW TO RISE TO THE TROT

The posting trot (also known as the "rising" trot) is easier and less tiring than the sitting trot for a beginner to master, so it should be taught first. Learning the posting trot is done more easily and efficiently on the lunge—so you don't have to worry about what the horse is doing or where it is going, and you can concentrate on getting used to and perfecting the technique. Rising to the trot is not as easy to accomplish as experienced riders make it look, so a novice should not feel disheartened if it's difficult to begin with. Until the necessary leg muscles for riding are toned and strong enough to cope, a novice's legs may feel—as one of my clients once described them—like useless lengths of limp string!

It is important not to work too hard at the posting trot, indeed you shouldn't need to at all. Using your upper legs and knees to stand up and then sit down in the saddle is not how it should be done. Doing this will make the exercise hard for you, plus you'll still be left behind the horse's movement. Rising and sitting is done in time to the trot beat: you will feel, and possibly hear, the "one, two, one, two, one, two…" rhythm as the horse's feet touch the ground in diagonal pairs. Repeat that constant and regular beat in your head, under your breath, or even out loud, and then attempt to move up and down in time to it.

Allow the horse's own movement to help lift your seat automatically in time to the beat, and allow your lower legs and heels to help you rise (though be aware that correct rising is not achieved by "standing" in the stirrups). Incline forward slightly from the hips on rising, without rounding the back, so that you stay in balance and with the movement. You should lift your seat only slightly out of the saddle—do not exaggerate the movement and stand right up allowing acres of daylight to be seen between your bottom and the saddle—so you do not get left behind the movement. Allow your hips to rise up and forward, then allow them to sink back down into the saddle again.

When you sit after rising, do so gently and squarely on both seatbones. Do not "thump" back down into the saddle as this won't do either the saddle or the horse's back any good at all. If your knees are stiff, this may pose a problem, so do try and let them relax and soften, allowing your lower legs and ankles to take the strain.

Hold the neckstrap, horse's mane, or the pommel to steady and balance yourself until you have learned the posting trot—do not use the reins as a lifeline to hold on to.

RISING ON THE CORRECT DIAGONAL

Riding in an arena, the rider should "sit on the correct diagonal," that is, the rider should be sitting when the horse's outside foreleg comes to the ground and rising when it's lifted forward.

To change diagonal, sit for two beats, instead of one, and then commence rising again. Eventually you will be able to feel when you are on the wrong diagonal, but beginners can check visually by glancing down at the horse's outside foreleg to see if they are sitting (incorrect) or rising (correct) when it moves forward. Help yourself sit correctly by saying "now" each time the outside foreleg comes to the ground, sitting when you say "now" and rising when you don't.

Remember to change the trot diagonal as you change the direction of the rein. On diagonal changes of rein you can change at X (the mark in the center of the arena), as you alter the horse's flexion (the bend of the horse's head), or on approach to the corner just before the rein change. Change diagonal frequently while riding so that the horse does not become one-sided.

RIDER'S POSITION
In order to remain secure in the saddle and absorb bounce in the sitting trot (and the canter), the rider's pelvic area should be relaxed and allowed to feel and follow the movement. It's almost a rocking sensation. Try this out of the saddle first: stand tall and relaxed, with your feet one to two feet (30 to 60 cm) apart, and knees slightly bent and relaxed. Roll your pelvis forward, up, back, and down. It may take a while but you should get this quite easily.

RISING ON THE DIAGONAL

The rider is on the left diagonal. As the horse's left forefoot hits the ground, the rider sits, then rises as the leg comes up and goes forward. When trotting on the left rein (see page 54), the rider should be sitting on the right diagonal; on the right rein, on the left diagonal. This is to help the horse balance more effectively when working on a circle and negotiating corners.

HOW TO SIT TO THE TROT

Learning to sit to the trot is most effectively done, as with rising, first on the lunge, to enable the rider to relax and concentrate on position without having to control the horse at the same time. Working without stirrups can help develop the supple and secure seat needed for sitting trot, but only at first for short spells of the trot. Hook your forefingers under the pommel to steady yourself to start with.

The most important element in being able to sit comfortably to the trot is having a well-balanced and independent seat, along with relaxed knees and legs.

Allow your hips, pelvic area, lower back, and knees to absorb the bounce. Sitting stiffly on the horse with your buttocks and knees tense will exacerbate the problem. Let yourself flow with the horse's movement, not on top of or against it.

Remember you can take hold of the horse's mane or neckstrap if you feel the need to steady yourself, but never use the reins as an anchor. Remember also to breathe! If you feel panicky at any time, make yourself take 10 deep breaths and you'll feel yourself physically and mentally calming down and relaxing.

Keep count of the horse's two-time trot beat in your head, and you will probably find that this helps you relax and move with the rhythm of the horse's movement: one, two, one, two, one, two, one, two… and so on.

AIDS FOR THE TROT

- Check that the walk is active, with sufficient impulsion for a transition (change of pace), and that the horse is listening to you (i.e. is ready, willing, and able) by applying a half-halt, or as many as you deem necessary to gain the horse's full attention (as described on page 24). The half-halt also prepares him for your command.

brace for a downward transition. The hands should be still in all transitions and should not grab at the horse's mouth nor collapse onto its neck and lose contact.

- To ask your horse for a downward transition to the walk, first half-halt, then lighten your weight in the saddle, and close your legs on its sides to support it. Think walk! Use a voice aid if necesssary. If the horse doesn't respond, try again.

- Be aware that when the horse does return to the walk, you must be ready to give instantly with your hands to allow its head and neck movement. But take care not to give so much that you lose control. "Throwing the reins at the horse" will confuse it and cause a loss of balance.

- If riding in an arena, check you have correct flexion (the bend of the horse's head) to the inside (see page 62) and that you have contact with the horse's mouth (this should, as always, be light—never "holding").

- Allow a little more weight into your seat and squeeze behind the girth with both lower legs and your horse should move forward smoothly into trot.

- Maintain the pace with your seat, weight, and legs. Keep your legs close to the horse's sides, but not squeezing or nudging constantly otherwise the horse will either go faster or soon begin to ignore them. Use your legs to nudge or squeeze only when necessary to maintain pace or apply an aid.

- Take care not to tip back as the horse moves into the trot, or forward as it slows to the walk again. If you do either, it means that you are tense—so relax. Use your back muscles to brace yourself for an upward transition and your abdominal muscles to

ABOVE Rising to the trot will be difficult if the stirrup leathers are too long. Here the rider is finding it hard to rise out of the saddle, resulting in a stiff posture.

QUESTION TIME

Q: *I find that in the posting trot my horse keeps trotting faster and faster, despite my efforts to control the pace. How can I prevent this?*

A: Count "one… two… one… two…" in your head at the speed you wish the trot to be and maintain rising and sitting to that beat—your horse will slow down to match it. It may feel uncomfortable and "out of sync" to you at first, but it does work. The same principle in reverse usually works for the opposite problem too, i.e. the horse slowing down. Also use half-halts to check your horse and regain its full attention.

Remember not to sit down heavily in the saddle or lean too far forward, because this can encourage the horse to go faster. Finally, ensure you are not tensing up nor gripping with the legs. A tense rider alarms a horse which will naturally want to get away from the "danger zone," while leg gripping is asking for an increase in pace.

Q: *When my instructor tells me to do a transition at a letter, where exactly should I do it—when the horse's nose reaches the letter or when my body reaches it?*

A: To be technically correct (as in a dressage test), a transition at a letter should be performed as the rider's shoulder comes level with it.

Q: *How fast does a horse go in the trot?*

A: It depends on the size of the animal and the length of its strides, so the speed can be anything from three miles (5 km) an hour up to 10 or 12 (16 or 19).

Q: *I always seem to get a "stitch" in my side when trotting. How can I prevent this?*

A: As soon as you feel a "stitch" tell your instructor, who should then direct you to walk and halt if necessary so that you can recover. It is caused by a muscle cramp, therefore stretching, flexing, and kneading the affected area may help. As you become riding fit and toned, the occurrence of "stitches" will lessen.

TAKING STOCK

Novice riders generally feel it necessary to hunch up in trot in an effort to feel more secure. However, doing this has the opposite effect; a "curled" upper body greatly reduces effectiveness of the seat and overall security, because as you allow your legs and feet to ride up, you become top-heavy. This makes you unbalanced and likely to fall off the horse. The more you can relax your legs, the more stable your seat will be. Also, avoid looking down—it's a nervous reaction that only serves to tense up your body. Look ahead and think positively.

Accomplishing a smooth and comfortable position and technique in both the posting and the sitting trot may take more than a few lessons, so be patient and persevere. Virtually everyone manages to achieve both sooner or later, so don't think that you never will! Remember that the ability to sit to the trot is an essential prerequisite for canter work.

SELF-HELP

- Spend time watching experienced riders trot, rising and sitting. Identify how they position themselves in the saddle and how they maintain a rhythm when rising. Watch how they apply aids and how the horse responds to them, and they to the horse.

- Seeing mistakes made by others is an excellent way of endeavoring to not do the same thing yourself.

BELOW Looking down causes the rider to lose his or her sense of direction, position, and, because he or she will be heavier in the saddle, makes the horse increase speed.

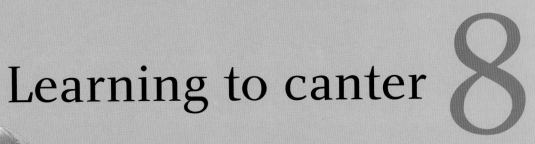

Learning to canter 8

LEFT This is where the real fun starts!

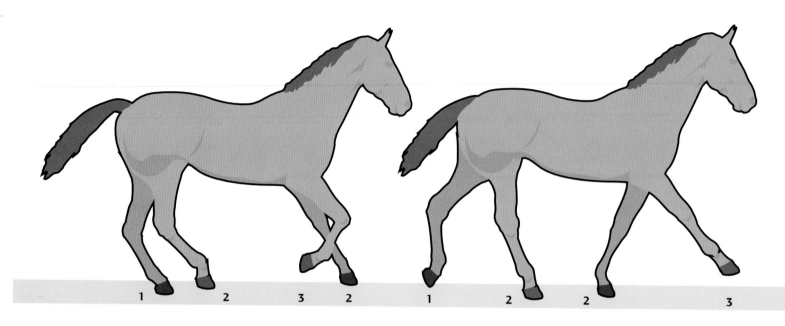

ABOVE The sequence of a horse's footfalls at the canter on the left rein. The outside hindleg should always begin the pace.

TOP The canter sequence of footfalls in action, with right foreleg leading.

When you have got the idea, the canter is, in my opinion, the most comfortable pace for a rider to sit to. It is a beautiful, rhythmical pace you could easily sit to all day! If likened to a dance, the canter could be termed a waltz (with the trot being the "foxtrot"!). Whether that waltz is a lively or stately one depends on the tempo (speed) of pace required.

HOW THE HORSE MOVES AT THE CANTER

The canter is a three-time movement, meaning that a hindleg strikes off first followed by a diagonal pair of front and hindlegs, and lastly by a foreleg. There is a brief moment of suspension when all four feet are off the ground at the same time.

In an arena, you will be told to ask your horse to strike off with the inside foreleg leading; for example "canter on the left or right leg." This instruction is given out so that the horse can balance itself as it goes around corners. On a straight line it does not matter which foreleg leads.

FACTS ABOUT THE CANTER

- As it canters, the horse's head and neck "nod" slightly in order to maintain balance, so the rider's arms and hands must move to accommodate this. If they don't, the rider will alternately jab the horse's mouth and lose contact.

- "Countercanter" is when a horse canters with the outside ("wrong") foreleg leading around an arena or in a circle. It is an advanced movement used to help build and improve a horse's athletic ability; it can also be used by a teacher at a certain stage in a client's progress to test their co-ordination and understanding of aids.

TYPES OF CANTER

As a beginner, you will practice in the "working" canter, otherwise referred to as the "active" canter. Other types of the canter are "medium," "collected," and "extended"—types you will learn as your riding progresses to a more advanced level than this book covers. The working canter should be active and freely

2   1   2   3   Moment of suspension

ABOVE The sequence of a horse's footfalls at the gallop (with the right foreleg leading); a four-time gait with a moment of suspension.

performed with a regular rhythm and constant pace. It should also feel balanced with a "swing" to it, which denotes that the horse is happy, relaxed and has sufficient impulsion. A lazy canter feels heavy, wooden, and "lumpy," and is extremely uncomfortable to sit to.

Some horses are naturally bouncier than others, which can make life difficult for a beginner, so it is preferable that a novice learns on a steady and comfortable horse. For the sake of both horse and rider, it is sensible for a novice rider to be taught the aids while maintaining position for the canter on the lunge. A well-trained horse whose transition to, and rhythm in, the canter is smooth and unrushed is the best tool with which to provide a novice with feel for the pace.

THE RIDER'S POSITION

The same principles apply as for the walk (see page 58).

THE "HALF" SEAT FOR THE CANTER

Also called the "forward," "jumping," or "cross-country" seat, this is where the rider inclines forward slightly, with the seat out of the saddle. It is used for a variety of purposes: When the rider wishes to reduce weight on the horse's back; for ease of rider and horse when cantering or galloping across open country; when jumping; or when a rider is saddlesore.

For this seat, it is the lower legs, knees, and inner thighs that support the rider's body weight and absorb bounce or shock. It is important not to hang onto the horse's mouth via the reins to help maintain balance.

HOW TO SIT TO THE CANTER

Do these exercises off the horse.

- Stand up straight, but relaxed, with your feet 12 to 18 inches (30 to 45 cm) apart.
- Look ahead.
- Bend your knees and keep them relaxed.
- Put your hands on the side points of your pelvic bones, just below your waist (some people say these are your hips but those are further down—at the top of your legs).
- Allow your knees to "give." Allow your seat

and pelvis to drop down, then push them forward slightly and up, and back and down; repeat over and over.

- Do not allow your shoulders and back to "rock"—let your lower back and seat area do all the work.

AIDS FOR THE CANTER

- It's essential that the trot is active, with sufficient impulsion for a transition, and that the horse is fully attentive to you. Remember those half-halts to maintain that attention and to prepare the horse for your actual canter request.
- If appropriate, e.g., in an arena, check that you have correct flexion and appropriate tension on the rein contact.
- If rising, sit to the trot a few strides before the point where you want, or have been instructed, to canter.
- Allow a little more weight into your seat

and squeeze behind the horse's girth with both lower legs and your horse should move forward smoothly into the canter. If it doesn't, but goes into a faster trot instead, then slow the trot speed down until you are happy it is balanced and rhythmic before applying the canter aid again. Do not panic and try to keep pushing the horse on into canter; this will simply make the problem worse. You will become flustered, as will the horse, and both of you will end up unbalanced and out of sync.

- To canter in an arena or in a circle, the inside leg should be applied on the girth to support the animal and ask for the correct leading foreleg to strike off, while the outside leg is applied just behind the girth to ask for forward movement into the canter and to prevent the quarters from swinging out too far. The inside hand asks for correct bend, while the outside hand maintains course and stops the horse from

BELOW Far left shows the correct riding position for the canter; the horse's head nods slightly in the canter, so the rider's hands should follow this movement to allow it freedom to move correctly, and to avoid pulling and losing contact with the horse's mouth. Center and right demonstrate incorrect positions for the canter; too far forward and too far back in the seat.

over-bending to the inside, as well as helping to check and control speed.

- Ensure that as the horse moves forward into the canter, you allow it to do so with your hands. Remember, your arms and hands should follow the movement of the horse's head and neck. What you must not do is keep your hands still and let your shoulders move instead to compensate, otherwise you will end up rocking backward and forward.

- Just as you do in the trot, maintain the pace with your seat, weight, and legs. Keep your legs close to the horse's sides, but not squeezing or nudging constantly, otherwise the horse will either go faster or soon begin to ignore them. Use your legs to nudge or squeeze only when necessary to maintain pace or apply an aid.

- Take care not to tip back as the horse moves into the canter, forward as it slows to the trot again—use your back and

ABOVE Take care when cantering in company that you do not allow a race to develop that may get out of control.

abdominal muscles to brace yourself appropriately, without stiffening up.

- To ask for a downward transition to the trot, simply half-halt, lighten your weight in the saddle slightly and apply your legs gently to support the horse. Think trot, and use a voice aid if necessary. If the horse doesn't respond, try again. The important thing is to not let yourself become anxious because that breeds tension.

- As the horse returns to the trot, remember to keep your hands still.

QUESTION TIME

Q: *I find that when I ask my horse to canter, it just trots faster and faster. How do I stop this happening and achieve a smooth transition into the canter?*
A: Remember to not look down, sit down heavily in the saddle, or hunch up and lean too far forward, because all of these actions can encourage the horse to go faster. Gripping up with the legs not only gives strong leg aids that

ABOVE Done correctly, the canter should be a controlled and smooth pace enjoyed by horse and rider alike.

signal "more speed", but this action also serves to communicate tension to the horse, who will automatically switch to "flight" instinct and do just that!

Novice riders often panic when an upward transition doesn't go as planned and find themselves urging the horse on faster in an effort to make it change pace into the one required. This only serves to unbalance both parties, with the rider losing position and control. If a transition doesn't happen, it's no big deal! You have all the time in the world to slow things down, take stock, and try again once you have rebalanced both yourself and the horse. The worst scenario is that your pride may be a little bruised, or you'll feel embarrassed for not being able to make the horse respond as you wanted it to, but again you must not let that be a problem. Remember, mind over matter! Take a deep breath, think positively, and repeat the exercise.

Q: *Should I shorten my reins for a transition?*
A: It should not be necessary if you maintain good rein contact at all times. However, at first, beginners often find their reins getting longer and longer until they discover the correct "feel" with the horse's mouth.

Q: *I bounce up and down in the canter. How can I stop myself doing this?*
A: Refer to "How to sit to the canter," page 74. Bouncing is a real problem for many beginners, especially if they are stiff, but it will get better if you practice my "special exercise"—I promise!

Q: *How fast does a horse move in the canter and in the gallop?*
A: Depending on the size, type, and fitness of the animal, and the length of its strides, canter speeds are between approximately three to 15 miles (4.8 to 24 km) an hour, while the gallop is 10 to 40 miles (16 to 64 km) an hour (there is quite a massive difference between a small pony and a champion racehorse!).

TAKING STOCK

As with the trot, novice riders often feel the necessity to hunch up in the canter in an effort to feel more secure; however doing this has the opposite effect because you become top-heavy. Refer back to "Taking stock" on page 70 for advice on how to relax.

If you find that you are having real problems with the canter, you should go back a step or two and work more on the walk and the trot to re-establish your balance, feel, and understanding of the aids. Sometimes, especially if a beginner seems to be progressing well, an instructor may assume the client can achieve more than he or she is ready for, or confident enough to attempt.

SELF-HELP

• As with the trot, it is very useful to spend some time watching experienced riders canter to see exactly how they position themselves in the saddle and move with the horse. Pay particular attention to how they use their pelvis and seat in that "rolling" action, which can seem so elusive to a beginner.

• Note where riders stop rising and sit to the trot before asking for a trot-to-canter transition (change of pace)—because a yard or two can make all the difference to a beginner rider in initial canter experiences.

• Watch how horses respond to their riders' aids. Was an aid given too strongly, too lightly, or just right?—you can tell a lot from a horse's reaction.

• Practice dismounted exercises whenever you get the chance, such as rotating wrists and ankles, tensing and relaxing leg muscles, and waist twists right and left, all serve to strengthen muscles and keep you toned and supple, ready for riding.

BELOW Gripping with the knees, as this rider demonstrates, leads to loss of balance. Tension in the rider is communicated to the horse, which invariably goes faster—leading to a loss of control on the rider's part.

HOW THE HORSE MOVES AT THE GALLOP

The gallop is a four-time movement, with the horse's legs moving in the following sequence: one hindfoot; the other hindfoot; forefoot on side of first hindfoot; forefoot on side of second hindfoot. There is a moment of suspension when all four feet are off the ground at the same time.

RIDING A HORSE AT THE GALLOP

Beginners won't be galloping for some considerable time, so it is not something you should worry about when you start riding. It is only when your instructor is happy that you can control a horse in the walk, trot, and canter, and so are you, that the opportunity to have a gallop may arise. Position-wise, you use the half-seat (see page 73). This is because it is more comfortable for both horse and rider, and helps balance both properly.

STOPPING A HORSE IN AN EMERGENCY

Using the "emergency stop" is unlikely to prove necessary for properly taught riders on suitable horses. It is extremely rough on the horse's mouth and can cause severe damage to it, so never use it unless you absolutely have to. With luck you won't ever have to use it, but if the situation arises where your horse is bolting or you need to stop a fast-moving horse quickly to avoid an accident, here's what you should do:

- Maintain normal riding position, sitting square in the saddle. Do not lean forward. Have the reins in both hands.
- Place one hand, rein in hand and knuckles down, firmly into the base of the horse's neck, just in front of the withers, and keep it there.
- Pull the horse's head around with the other hand and hold it there—you may have to use all your strength for this.
- Lean back, push your lower legs forward, and brace both your back and abdominal muscles. When the horse stops it will be sharply, and this position will help stop you from flying over its shoulder.

BELOW At the gallop the rider should adopt a forward position with the seat out of the saddle, as shown, to avoid being left behind the movement.

Learning to jump 9

LEFT It is in situations like this that a rider appreciates why it is so necessary to learn the basic skill of independent balance on a horse from the outset. Although in a precarious position, this rider is not worried nor is he hampering his horse in any way, because he is confident in his ability to balance and move with his horse upon landing—and ride on to the next obstacle.

"Jumping"— the word probably has both an exciting and scary ring to it for you, the beginner. From the outset be reassured that jumping over obstacles is not as difficult as you might imagine, and it is a source of enormous fun when approached in a proper and sensible way.

JUMP TO IT!

Basically, jumping entails getting from one side of an obstacle over to the other. That obstacle may only be an inch or two off the ground initially, and up to several feet later in your riding career when you are confident and capable enough to tackle such a height. To build up confidence, it's essential that you do not allow yourself to be rushed or pushed into attempting anything that may scare you. Confidence-building may take only a matter of months, depending on your ability and temperament, or it may take years. However long it takes, your goal is to be comfortable and happy when jumping, if that's what you want to do.

Some people feel pressured into jumping by fellow riders when in fact they may not want to leave the ground one little bit. If this is you,

then ignore the others and concentrate on your own enjoyment of riding in the way you like most. Just because you do not want to jump does not mean you are a failure. Many top equestrian riders, in their chosen sports that do not involve jumping, such as dressage, are testament to the fact that you don't have to jump to be a good and sympathetic rider. It's better to have the good sense to realize that jumping makes you nervous, or you do not enjoy it at all, than risk injuring yourself and

BELOW No thank you!

BELOW RIGHT Showing fine style. Even though take-off was a little too far away from the fence, horse and rider have recovered well and are straining every muscle to clear the obstacle.

INTO ACTION—HORSE AND RIDER JUMPING POSITIONS

your horse. Worrying about "what others might think" is a negative emotion and one that will hamper your riding progress, so do not give in to it!

If you are the type of person who approaches jumping with a natural confidence, you'll more than likely get a real "buzz" from this discipline and progress quickly. If you are more cautious about the prospect, you will find your confidence boosted enormously by an understanding and able instructor. There is nothing difficult about jumping once you are able to position yourself correctly in the saddle and understand the actions and movements of the horse when it approaches and jumps over an obstacle. The important thing to remember is that if you can keep your balance and position over a small obstacle only a couple of inches off the ground, then bigger fences will present no problem. As fences get bigger, it is the rider who is usually afraid of jumping them, not the horse. It is when progressing to jumping that the rider truly realizes what power the mind has over the body.

Although horses are not specifically designed to jump obstacles, they can do it with aplomb—and many really enjoy the job, tackling the most massive of obstacles with great relish. If they didn't want to do it, they wouldn't, and no effort on a rider's part would force them to do it.

Using the illustration as a guide, note how the horse's shape changes as it accomplishes the different stages of jumping. After landing, the getaway stage is known as "recovery." Now look again and see how the rider is positioned to move with the horse in order to help it jump the obstacle by not hindering it in any way. You can see how the rider adjusts his or her center of gravity to stay central as the horse's center of gravity changes during the jump. Not to do this would result in the rider becoming unbalanced and probably falling off. Importantly, see how the rider's hands follow the stretching movement of the horse's head and neck to allow the horse freedom to use its body efficiently. If

ABOVE Jumping positions–approach, take-off, moment of suspension over the jump, descent, and landing.

Learning to jump

the rider's hands stayed fixed in position, then they would not allow the horse's body to assume the necessary shape in order for it to jump over the obstacle comfortably.

Being able to assume the correct jumping position and flow of movement during each stage of jumping improves with practice.

JUMPING POSITION

This is really quite simple. Apart from shortening the stirrups a hole or two, you maintain normal riding position (whether it be in the trot or the canter) on approach to a jump to maintain the horse's impulsion. If you approach in the posting trot, take the sitting trot a few strides away from the jump so that your seat is secure and you are ready for take-off. It is only at the moment of take-off that you need to incline forward from the hips in order to remain over the horse's center of gravity, with your seat staying in the saddle and your back flat, not rounded. To maintain contact allow your hands and arms to follow the horse's head and neck as they stretch forward. Your lower legs, knees, and thighs provide the support you need to remain secure and balanced in the saddle. Remember to keep your knees relaxed; if allowed to stiffen they will hamper your ease of movement and reduce your lower leg security.

During the moment of suspension you will still be inclined forward, beginning to return to an upright position on descent in readiness for the landing and getaway.

On descent, the horse's head and neck will "retract," and as this happens your hands and arms should begin to return to their normal

position so that contact is maintained at all times. But be ready to give or take contact with your hands as necessary should the horse stumble on landing (so you must "give" and support him between yours hands and legs) or try to charge off (in which case you must "take" contact).

On landing, you should be upright again in readiness for the getaway. It is on landing that you discover why it is so important to have relaxed knees and an upright position. If you are still leaning forward and your knees are tense, you will find yourself being catapulted out of the saddle over the horse's head or shoulder. With soft knees and an upright posture you can absorb the shock of landing easily, and recover your position quickly in order to maintain controlled forward movement. Sometimes you may find that you have to give contact away fully (known as "slipping the reins") on landing or getaway if the horse gets into difficulty. This lets the horse find and regain its own balance without interference from you.

It is only over large fences that it is necessary for the rider's seat to be brought out of the saddle because of the extra effort needed in moving with the horse to stay over its center of gravity. Refer back to Chapter Eight, "The half-seat" on page 73, for advice on how to achieve this position.

FROM THE BEGINNING

Usually beginners start their jumping lessons over trotting poles (also known as ground poles). These are long poles placed on the ground, set apart at distances appropriate to the horse's length of trot stride. The idea of this exercise is to get the rider used to the horse

ABOVE Using weight, seat, and leg aids and, importantly, looking in the direction she wants to go, this rider is directing her horse, in preparation for going over trotting poles, without the use of reins.

OPPOSITE Midway through an obstacle and this rider is already looking toward the next, showing complete confidence in what she is doing and where she wants to go.

picking its feet up higher than normally, and also to practice aiming for the center of the obstacles.

Position-wise, negotiating the poles in walk or trot is exactly the same as if you were riding on the flat. You just have to be more attentive in maintaining pace, tempo, and rhythm, otherwise the horse may trip and stumble over the poles. Looking ahead is essential to maintaining your position, therefore ensuring you ride a straight line. Riding over ground poles in "jumping position," i.e. leaning forward slightly as you would on take-off, helps you tone and strengthen appropriate muscles to hold this position easily, and it also accustoms you to the feel of the horse "bouncing" more off the ground.

Riding a straight line over the poles is excellent practice for when you begin jumping for real. If a horse decides it can save effort by going around the obstacle, it will do so; therefore it is up to the rider to ensure the horse doesn't by simultaneously aiming for the center of the obstacle and applying appropriate aids.

WHAT JUMPING ACTUALLY FEELS LIKE

Once you have mastered trotting poles, the next step is leaving the ground over small jumps only a few inches high. The step from going over poles on the ground to poles off the ground is quite a major one for a beginner. This is where you'll understand why the neckstrap is such a good friend to you and your horse. It's a safety handle for you, and therefore helps prevent you pulling on the reins and jabbing your horse in the mouth.

A horse will take bouncy strides over ground poles, but it will "hop" over a small jump. Nothing you have encountered so far has prepared you for this movement, so you will more than likely be taken by surprise and the movement will feel both bumpy and uncomfortable. For the first couple of jumps, hold on to that neckstrap for extra stability until you can anticipate the movement and judge how to move your body with it. Practice makes perfect, and sooner or later you will discover the key to moving easily and comfortably while staying in balance with the horse.

Ideally, your first lessons over trotting poles and small jumps should be on the lunge, so that you can concentrate fully on keeping your balance and position without having to worry about guiding the horse and maintaining its forward movement. Once you have mastered position over jumps, you will then find it easier to control the horse at the same time.

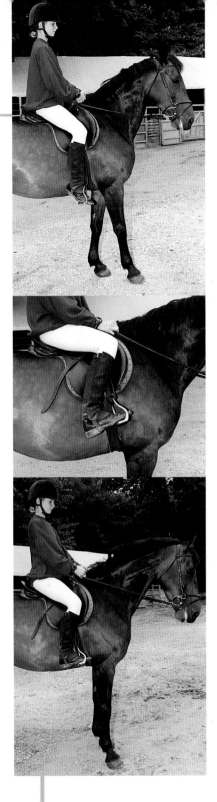

STIRRUP LENGTH
Having the correct stirrup length is essential when jumping: Too long (top) and the rider will be reaching for them and be unbalanced; too short (middle) and the rider will be top heavy and liable to bounce out of the saddle. The bottom picture shows the correct position.

ABOVE In trouble over a fence; this rider has "slipped the reins" to let her horse find and regain its balance, without jabbing it in the mouth, while she maintains her own equilibrium.

As you become more proficient over single jumps, you can then move on to tackling small courses of two, three, and more fences. The golden rule here is to always look where you are going. As you are negotiating one jump, look to see where the next one is positioned. Your brain and body will respond to the challenge of guiding your horse to and over it. On landing, you cannot afford to relax; you must maintain control and impulsion whether there is another fence to jump or not. If you lose your concentration, your horse will naturally take advantage of your loss of control.

As you progress to jumping larger fences, you will find them easier to negotiate than you perhaps expected—as long as you have mastered the basic balance and co-ordination. If you can jump small fences in balance and in comfort, bigger ones will present no problems to you. You will not fall off because you have mastered the basic seat and position, and the feeling of flying smoothly over a nice big fence is absolutely wonderful—there's nothing quite like it!

SELF-HELP

• While in halt practice inclining (also known as "folding") forward as if on take-off. Sit tall, look ahead, allow your inner thigh muscles and pelvic area to relax, and fold forward from the hips, not the waist. Keep your back flat and think of your chin touching the horse's mane in front of you. This exaggerates the incline, but it will give you a clear idea of the movement desired.

• Another tip you'll find helpful is to think of "pushing" your stomach, chest, and shoulders down toward your horse's withers. As you incline forward, allow your hands to travel forward as if following a horse's outstretched head and neck, without resting them on its neck. Remember to keep your knees relaxed, letting your weight travel down into your lower legs, which will secure your seat position. Then slowly bring yourself upright again, using only your abdominal and back muscles to do so.

• Once you have got the feel of those movements with your body and hands in halt, try them in walk, then trot, and finally canter. Keep practicing until you have perfected the movements and are keeping your balance in all three paces. The end result of your inclining forward and then coming upright again should be a fluid, smooth movement, not a jerky and hesitant one. Practice doing it faster and faster; this will stand you in good stead for the speed at which the movement is required when actually going over jumps.

• It is essential that you do not tip to one side as you fold forward, otherwise you will unbalance yourself and the horse. Think of keeping your spine in line with the horse's.

• Watch expert riders jump—you can learn a lot from doing this. See how they position themselves in the saddle and how they approach jumps. Watch how they fold at the moment of take-off and how they straighten up again on descent and landing.

BELOW LEFT Although this horse has made a mistake jumping up and out of water, the rider is positioned well enough to help the horse regain its equilibrium and remain on its feet.

BELOW MIDDLE Sometimes falls are unavoidable, but they rarely result in serious harm to horse or rider.

BELOW RIGHT If the rider tips too far forward on take-off, as here, and then during suspension, it can result in the horse becoming unbalanced and the rider being unable to achieve correct position on landing. This can have the effect of the horse stumbling on landing and the rider falling off over its head.

TAKING STOCK SO FAR— JUMPING PROBLEMS

You are likely to encounter some problems with jumping. These may include: Not being able to maintain position; stiffening up; feeling nervous, which results in tension; finding it difficult to feel just how much contact to give and take; maintaining impulsion; keeping your legs still and stopping them from gripping up or moving back; stopping your horse from motorbiking around a corner in its haste to get at a jump; and maintaining pace rhythm. Don't worry about these problems. Every rider encounters them, and worrying about them only makes the situation worse. Anxiety is a negative emotion, sapping confidence and making small problems into larger ones, so banish worries and don't let them hamper your progress. Instead of fretting about a problem, examine it and try to think what the problem stems from. This is a positive and constructive action, taking your mind off the problem itself and instead looking for a solution.

Your instructor is there to help you overcome problems, so never be afraid or reluctant to ask for advice. If you don't understand the method explained to you, then say so in order that your teacher can try to explain or show you in a different way, one that makes more sense to you.

If you decide you really do not like jumping and feel uncomfortable with it, again you must tell your instructor. Not saying anything indicates acceptance. Your instructor is not a mind reader and cannot be expected to know what you are thinking or feeling. It is far better to state categorically that you do not want to jump, than to allow yourself to be miserable during lessons and begin to dread them. Riding should provide enjoyment for you, not be a form of torture!

QUESTION TIME

Q: *I have heard fences being referred to as "rider frighteners." What does this mean?*
A: Some fences (especially on cross-country courses) are designed to scare a rider, but they are in fact extremely inviting from a horse's

point of view—hence the term "rider frightener." If a rider can learn to assess a fence from a horse's point of view, many rider frighteners will cease to earn their name.

Q: *How high can horses jump?*
A: It depends on the size and build of animal. The weight and conformation of heavily built horses and short-legged and chunky ponies do not lend themselves to athletic ability over sizable obstacles.

The official world equestrian high jump record was set in 1949 by the Chilean rider Captain Alberto Larraguibel Morales on Huaso, who jumped eight feet one-and-a-half inches (2.48 m). In the same year, a jump of eight feet six inches (2.59 m) was recorded in Queensland, Australia, achieved by Jack Martin on Gold Meade, but this was not recognized officially because it was not performed while competing.

ABOVE Common position faults while jumping: too far forward (left) and too far back (right).

BELOW Even the best come unstuck sometimes, as top New Zealand event rider Andrew Nicholson demonstrates. Known for his amazing "stickability" in the saddle, this fall was a rare occurrence for Andrew. Horse and rider were unhurt.

Going it alone 10

LEFT There's nothing quite like the feeling of being at one with your horse, knowing you are competent enough to deal with any awkward situations that may arise.

Going it alone

The length of time between your first riding lesson and being competent enough to ride out alone may seem to be forever. For many novices, the lure of being able to take a horse out riding alone in the countryside is almost overwhelming—and frustrating too until that magic moment finally arrives.

THINKING FOR YOURSELF

Riding out alone, and in company, is vastly different than riding in an enclosed arena with your instructor close by to give advice and lend a helping hand when necessary. When out alone you have to think for yourself and your horse all the time, be on your guard and aware of what's happening around you every single moment.

Out of a familiar and safe environment, a horse will feel vulnerable, its senses will be heightened ready to take action, that is to say, run off if anything it perceives as danger threatens it. So, while riding out is huge fun, you must be able to control your mount safely to ensure that it does not present a hazard to pedestrians and road users encountered on your ride.

ABOVE Riding out with a friend or two for company is safer than going out alone because there'll be someone to go for help should an accident occur. Carrying a mobile phone is a good idea too, although some horses can be frightened by its ringing tone.

BOTTOM LEFT The correct and easiest way to carry a saddle.

BOTTOM MIDDLE AND RIGHT Stirrups should be secured correctly when leading a horse.

TACKING UP

PUTTING THE BRIDLE ON
The best way of learning how to put on and take off a bridle (and saddle) is for someone to show you how to do it.

- If the horse is tied up, undo the halter (headcollar) and refasten the headpiece around the horse's neck so that it cannot escape. Some halters have buckled nosebands; simply undo this. If the horse is loose in a stable or field, follow the instructions below.
- Ensure that the bridle's throatlatch (throat strap) and noseband are unbuckled.
- Put the reins over the horse's head, and loop your arm through the nearest one to stop the horse from wandering off.
- Standing facing in the same direction as the horse, put your right arm under its jaw and gently take hold of its nose halfway down its face. (Continued on page 90.)

PUTTING ON THE BRIDLE

Putting on a bridle, taking care not to catch the horse's eyes and ears.

To take off the bridle, leave the reins around the horse's neck with one arm threaded through so it cannot escape, undo the throatlatch and noseband, take hold of the headpiece, gently lift it over the horse's ears and drop it down allowing the horse to release the bit itself. Never drag the bit from the horse's mouth because you might hurt it or damage its mouth and teeth, and cause the animal, not surprisingly, to become headshy.

PUTTING ON THE SADDLE

Ensure the horse is safely tied up, that the saddle's stirrups are run up and secured and that the girth is placed over the saddle seat so it does not flap about and hurt or frighten the horse.

Place the saddle gently in front of the withers and slide it back into place just behind the shoulders. Never slide the saddle forward against the lay of the coat.

Attach the girth onto the first two right-hand saddle girth straps, then go around the front of the horse and fasten the girth on to the first two left-hand saddle girth straps. Ensure the girth straps are always on equal holes at the same height.

Gently, one hole at a time, tighten the girth enough to prevent the saddle from slipping. There should be enough "slack" for you to be able to slide a flat hand between the girth and the horse.

When mounted, and after warming up, check the girth's tightness again as some horses "blow" themselves out when their girths are being tightened.

Take down the stirrups only when you are ready to mount. Reverse to remove the saddle.

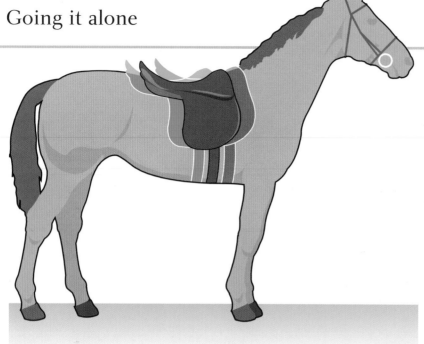

ABOVE Positioning the saddle. The illustration shows, from left to right, too far back, correct, and too far forward.

BELOW Tightening the girth while mounted.

- Hold the bridle by its cheekpieces with your right hand also, and lay the bit flat on your left hand.
- Lift the bridle with the right hand until the bit is touching the horse's lips.
- At this point some horses will open their mouths and allow you to slide the bit in gently while lifting the bridle up with the right hand to keep it in place. Some horses won't be so obliging, and you have to slide your left thumb into the corner of the mouth (there are no teeth here) to encourage the horse to open its mouth so you can slide the bit in.
- Once the bit is in, gently lift the bridle up and over the horse's ears, carefully moving the ears under the headpiece, and allow it to rest behind the ears.
- Gently rearrange the mane and forelock back into their rightful positions. The forelock should lie over the browband.

- Fasten the throatlatch first, allowing four fingers' space between it and the horse's gullet, and then the noseband, allowing space to fit two fingers between it and the horse's nose.

TOP TIPS

Ensure the bridle will fit the horse before attempting to put it on, by laying it full length against the animal's face from behind the ear to the jaw. The bit (where bit ring and mouthpiece join together) should reach to (not shorter or longer) the corner of the horse's mouth.

- If the bridle is too short between bit and headpiece, it will cause discomfort when trying to fit it. The horse may be reluctant for you to try again once you have adjusted the bridle. If the bridle is too large, the bit will simply hang out of the horse's mouth and be ineffective and uncomfortable.
- Adjust the cheekpieces to make the bridle's head size bigger or smaller as needed.
- A jointed bit should just wrinkle the corners of the lips, while a straight bit should touch the corners but not wrinkle them. On each side of the bit there should be space to fit one finger's width between the horse's lips and the bit ring.

RIDING ON ROADS

Riding on roads is something few riders can avoid these days due to limited opportunities for off-road riding in many areas. Because of ever-increasing traffic on roads today, the risks involved when riding horses on highways (and even supposedly quiet country roads) are high. Few horses are completely "traffic-proof;" many

will tolerate light traffic such as cars reasonably well, but high-sided vehicles and large trucks tend to scare them with their size and noise. Coupled with the fact that many motorists do not appreciate that horses are easily spooked by vehicles passing too close or too fast, road riding is extremely hazardous. Try to steer clear of busy roads.

Confine traffic schooling for your horse to a safe environment back home or at a training yard. Get off your horse and lead it past the obstacle it refuses to pass on a road and calm it down until the potential danger is behind.

When approaching an intersection, never go out into the middle of the road in preparation to turn across oncoming traffic. Stay by the side but signal your direction intent. For example, to turn left from one road to another, drivers will position themselves on the left side of their lane in preparation to turn. However if horse riders did this they would be placing themselves and their horses in an extremely vulnerable position. It is safer to stay right of the road so they can get out of the way more easily and safely if the need arises.

Do not ride on the sidewalk; it is for pedestrians only. However, it is safer to temporarily step onto the sidewalk—providing no pedestrians are in the vicinity and therefore at risk—than to remain obstructing or in danger of traffic.

RIDING IN THE COUNTRYSIDE

Accessible countryside is there for everyone to enjoy and the golden rule is to leave it as you found it.

COURTESY CODE TIPS

- If you pass through gates that were closed, fasten them securely behind you.
- Do not ride through livestock, especially at lambing or calving time; instead stay close to boundary fencing.
- Do not ride through crops; instead stay close to the boundary or designated trail.
- Do not damage fencing or gates.
- Always check with the landowner first before riding over land other than designated trails.
- If a trail is wet, do not churn it up by galloping along it; walk carefully.
- If you spot anything amiss, for example broken fencing or escaping stock, inform the landowner as soon as possible.

ABOVE LEFT When riding through fields containing livestock, always keep at walk and well away from the animals. Never ride over freshly sown fields of crops—keep to the edges or designated paths. Always check with the landowner that it is acceptable to ride over farmland.

ABOVE MIDDLE When out riding in the country, always remember to shut gates after going through to prevent livestock escaping.

ABOVE Whatever the weather and time of day, it is safer for the rider to wear a fluorescent vest when out riding on roads or country roads.

RIGHT A bucking horse.

- Do not take dogs with you on rides, no matter how well-behaved you consider yours to be. You cannot control them adequately on a long lead without risk of them wrapping themselves around your horse's legs, and if allowed to run loose they present a hazard to your horse, other livestock, road users, and people.
- Stay out of roadside ditches, which often conceal drains, rabbit holes, and various types of garbage.

PROBLEM-SOLVING

There are occasions when out riding that you may encounter behavioral problems with your horse. Providing you have been taught well, and use your common sense, you will probably find you can cope quite ably. The following problems are those most frequently encountered by riders.

BUCKING

Bucking is where the horse puts its head down in order to lift its hindlegs off the ground. The energy and "lift" of the buck combined with the balance and position of the rider determine whether the rider remains seated on the horse or not. Bucking is done for a variety of reasons: high spirits; playfulness; alarm (if something startles the animal); to dislodge the rider because the saddle or rider's position is hurting it, or because its back hurts for another reason; to dislodge the rider if it has learned that bucking is a good way of doing this.

If a horse has suddenly taken to bucking on a regular basis, its back should be checked for physical discomfort by a vet who specializes in horses. After that, a reputable saddle fitter should be called out to check the fit of the

saddle (with a rider sitting on it) to ensure it is not causing pain.

Care should be taken to ensure that saddle pads are fitted correctly and are not wrinkled or pressing on the spine, both of which will cause discomfort, and that the girth is not too tight and is free from lumps and tears because these can cause rubbing.

PREVENTING AND SITTING A BUCK

- Do not allow the horse to lower its head further than its knees. Do this by maintaining contact and forward movement, employing half-halts when necessary to hold its attention. A horse can only buck when its head is low enough for it to lift its hindquarters.
- If you feel a horse tense itself in preparation to buck, turn around and ride it onto a tight circle until you feel the tension go.

- Persistent buckers, especially small ponies that take advantage of their weak child riders, can be controlled with "grass reins"—lengths of strong string or cord that are fastened to the D-rings on each side of the pommel, run up each side of the pony's neck to and down through the browband loops and down to be fastened with quick-release knots (see Chapter 11 for how to tie these) on the bit rings. They should be long enough for normal head carriage and activity, but short enough to stop the animal getting its head down far enough to buck.

- It's not advisable to hit a horse with a stick when it bucks. First, you won't be able to do it quickly enough to make the horse associate bucking with being punished. Secondly, you'll need a hand free to smack the horse and this is easier said than done. Finally, smacking a horse often makes it buck all the more. Reprimand the animal with your voice, and concentrate on getting its head up and sending it forward calmly again. Many horses find it easier to buck when forward movement is not maintained, so ensure that it is maintained.

- To remain seated, lean back slightly, keep your heels down and lower legs forward, keep the knees soft and not gripped into the saddle (but not taken right off the horse) and look ahead.

REARING

A horse rears by lifting its front feet off the ground and standing on its hindlegs. It does this for the same reasons as for bucking, but mainly in serious alarm or resistance. Often a horse starts the habit by jibbing (see next page), and then takes it a step further by actually rearing. When a horse rears, or attempts to, lean your weight forward over its forehand to help push it back down and to remain balanced in the saddle. Strongly send the horse forward with your leg and voice. A horse cannot rear if its head and neck are flexed sideways, so if you feel a rear coming on turn the animal in a tight circle until you feel it calm down and willingly go forward again.

Never pull at the horse's mouth if it rears because you may end up pulling it over backward on top of you.

BELOW A rearing horse.

JIBBING

Jibbing is when a horse refuses to go forward and may walk or run backward to avoid doing so. As with bucking, the animal and its tack must be checked to ensure discomfort is not causing the problem. It may be that something has alarmed the animal, so you should check ahead for danger. In some cases horses have refused to move because their "sixth sense" has alerted them to danger ahead, and in refusing to go forward they have saved themselves and their riders from injury and even death. If a horse does not normally jib, take notice of what it is trying to tell you. A horse may feel insecure about going out alone, so you should reassure it by applying aids clearly and firmly, soothing it with your voice. If necessary, get off the animal and lead it for a while before remounting.

COPING WITH A JIBBER

- Circling the animal and firmly asking it to walk forward sometimes works. If it doesn't and there is no apparent reason for the horse jibbing, other than it being extremely stubborn, an expert rider will need to be called to school the animal.

NAPPING

A horse that refuses to comply with its rider's aids, or won't leave the yard on its own or without its stablemate, or won't pass certain places on rides is termed as being "nappy." There are many reasons for this behavior. A rider may be asking the horse to go forward with the legs but preventing it from doing so comfortably with the hands. A nervous rider may be transmitting fear to the horse, which will naturally not want to proceed if it senses fear in the rider. Insecurity, stubbornness, a nervous temperament, and lack of confidence could all lead to napping. Some horses will be alarmed by certain objects or shades of color, such as huge corn silos or bright white gates. The former are frighteningly big and therefore a "threat," and the latter may be affecting the horse's clarity of vision. A smell at a certain point on the ride may trigger alarm in a horse too, especially if it associates that smell with something unpleasant or scary that has happened in its past. Many horses are terrified of pigs for some reason, and refuse to go near pig farms.

COPING WITH NAPPING

- Circling the animal until you regain its attention, and therefore full control, and then sending it on forward can be effective.
- If there is a certain spot on a ride at which the horse naps strongly, try to avoid it.
- Dismounting and leading the horse past the frightening place may also work. Remount once you are past it.
- However, if the horse naps at anything and everything, and you cannot deal with it effectively and safely, you must seek expert help. Coping with nappy horses needs capable, determined, and strong riding; if you have a real problem then call in an expert to help you find a solution.
- Do not try to force the horse to go up to a place or object it is frightened of because this will just make the situation worse. Allow it, if it wants to, to approach it in its own good time to "check it out" and satisfy itself there is nothing to be alarmed about.

BELOW
Napping–refusing to move.

SHYING

Shying is when a horse suddenly moves sideways, frightened by something at the roadside or ahead of it. Causes can be a plastic bag blowing across the path, a bird suddenly rising noisily from the ground or bush, or a gunshot or car backfiring. As the movement of shying is often totally unexpected and sudden, it can be unseating as well as scary for the rider.

If you remember that a rider should be alert at all times and ready to apply aids as and when necessary, you will be better prepared to deal with a sudden shy. When you feel a potential shy coming, use your leg aids confidently and firmly, and allow the horse to go forward with your hands. If you feel the horse shying left, away from something on its righthand side, maintain strong pressure with the left leg to prevent further sideways movement and send it on strongly with the right leg, turning its head away from the "spook." The opposite applies if the horse shies to its right.

To educate young horses, some schools of thought advise letting the horse look at the object, and if this works for you and your horse then do this instead. In other circumstances, however, turning the horse's head toward a "scary" object can create further difficulties. If you feel it would be safer, then dismount and lead the animal past the problem spot, remounting further along the way. Horses that are habitually nervous and shy should not be ridden on roads, to avoid the real risk of accidents.

A rider can actually cause a shy by being nervous, and therefore transmitting fear to the horse. If a rider worries about, for example, an approaching vehicle that he or she thinks the horse will shy at, then the horse will sense that it is something to be scared of and shy away from it. An air of confidence is required when riding out, to avoid problems.

SELF-HELP

It is important to realize that once you have learned the basics of riding, i.e. being able to control your horse in all paces and over jumps under instruction, you should not stop having lessons—even if reduced to only once a month. Continuing to receive instruction, especially if you are lucky enough to have your own horse, is essential to improve your knowledge and practical ability, overcome problems you may encounter, and prevent you forming bad habits when you ride. Where horses are concerned, you never stop learning new methods, better ways of doing things, and, most importantly, increasing your depth of understanding of how the horse communicates, feels, and thinks.

RIDING OUT—TOP TIPS

- Avoid "racing" your horse with companions if you are not certain you will be able to stop when and where you want to.
- Avoid riding out with people who cannot stop their horses from charging off because this will excite your horse and may cause it to try and do the same, creating potential behavior problems.
- Always slow down and give way to oncoming pedestrians on a path—remember that horses frighten some people.

ABOVE Water can prove a great attraction for some horses. Some want to stand and have a splash, while others like to roll in it. Strong driving-forward aids, along with a sharp smack with the whip behind the leg perhaps, generally do the trick of preventing an impromptu bath.

- Always be courteous to motorists and other road users, especially when they slow down for you and pass with care. If you do not consider it safe to raise a hand and acknowledge their courtesy, a nod and a smile will do just as well. Never be rude to inconsiderate motorists and anyone else you may encounter on rides, as this creates bad feelings toward horse riders in general.

BELOW When riding in the country, beware of trash and holes in the ground on which a horse could injure itself and, as a result, the rider also.

QUESTION TIME

Q: *If a horse is being stubborn I have heard that you should not dismount or give in to it until you have made it behave, otherwise the horse will think it can get its own way and repeat the behavior the next time it's ridden. Is this true?*

A: It depends on the situation, and the rider's level of expertise and knowledge. In some cases it is safer and wiser to dismount and lead the horse past whatever it is objecting to. Or it might be sensible to stop trying to achieve the exercise that is upsetting the animal, or causing it to become stubborn, and do something else instead until it calms down. These actions are not giving in—the rider is being sensible and humane if the horse is genuinely scared or confused. A horse will remember the last thing it did, so it's important to end something on a good and pleasant note.

Where a rider is certain a horse is being deliberately stubborn, then it is prudent to continue to demand that the horse obey for its own good. However, the rider must be experienced enough, both mentally and physically, to cope with this training, otherwise the situation will worsen and the risk of injury will be heightened.

LEFT Before jumping an obstacle when out riding, always check what is on the other side first and that the landing is safe. Steep drops, big ditches, and tangles of wire are just some of the hazards that a rider could come across.

LEFT Owning a horse or pony is the ambition of many riders. However, you have to choose a suitable equine partner carefully. You must also be dedicated to its correct care and essential needs, for continued good mental and physical health, and enjoyment by both horse and rider.

Buying a horse is the easy part of actually owning one; the tricky part is finding the perfect equine partner. Horse ownership is not something that should be rushed into lightly or on a whim, for your sake and the animal's.

BUYING A HORSE

It is a sensible idea to take your instructor with you when looking at potential purchases. While you may be excited and keen to buy the first animal you see, your instructor will take a more critical and unbiased view, and will have the experience and knowledge to judge whether the horse will suit you, and you the horse. An instructor will also be able to ascertain if there are any obvious faults or problems with the animal and advise you accordingly. Although it may be expensive to take your instructor with you every time you look at a horse, it can be money well spent (and saved!) in the long run.

BELOW Finding somewhere to keep your horse needs careful thought. Keeping it at a boarding stable or riding establishment is the best option for a first-time owner because there'll be experienced help at hand should it be required as well as other horse owners with whom to socialize and ride.

PRE-PURCHASE PREPARATION

Before you even start looking for a horse to buy, there are essential details that must be sorted out first. Although you will be champing at the bit to go out and look at potential equine partners, it's no good if you buy one and then realize you haven't arranged the means to care for it properly.

- How much can you afford to pay? Your budget will determine what type of animal you can afford to look at. Include in your budget the cost of tack if you need to buy some, the cost of pre-purchase vetting (contact veterinarians to get quotes), insurance for you and your horse (call insurance companies and get estimates), the cost of transporting the horse, how much the instructor will charge for each horse viewing, the cost of inoculations (remember that these may not be up to date when you buy an animal) and worming, the first month's stable fees (or feed, hay, and bedding if you are keeping the horse at home), and shoeing (in case a new purchase needs shoeing as soon as you get it home).
- Where will you keep the horse? And where will you be able to ride it?
- You need to find a qualified farrier who is willing to shoe your horse.
- Find where the nearest veterinarian is who specializes in equines, and whether he or she has room on the patient list for you.
- Check out local horse hay, feed, and bedding suppliers, and compare prices and quality. You need to ensure you can always obtain those items.
- Find out about any local riding clubs.

- Discover where the nearest qualified and experienced instructors are so that you can call on them for help as and when required.
- You will also need to contact horse transport companies to get an idea of how much it will cost you to get a horse home (many charge by distance).

FACILITIES

If you keep horses at home you will need at least two acres (0.8 ha) of pasture per horse, which is free from poisonous plants, holes, debris, and implements that could injure your new equine companion. Pasture should be split into at least two good-sized paddocks so that one can be rested and cleared of weeds and dung while the other is grazed. The paddocks should be securely fenced, preferably post and rail rather than wire. I have found electric fencing to be particularly good at keeping horses at home; horses that push their way through post and rail tend to respect electric fencing. If you use electric fencing, you must ensure that grass under it isn't allowed to grow tall enough to touch the tape, rope, or wire, or it will break the connection at that point and render the rest of the fence useless. Batteries, if used, should be checked regularly. Test fences periodically—you can buy fence testers cheaply—to ensure they are working. Portable electric fencing is useful when splitting up paddocks, sectioning off turn-out areas in wet seasons to preserve the rest of the pasture, or creating limited grazing areas to slim down fat or laminitic horses (see "Horse Care" p. 105).

Your horse will need shelter from prevailing wind and rain, and this can be provided courtesy of a good thick hedge or a specially built field shelter. The use of a loose box (minimum size 12 feet by 12 feet (3.6 x 3.6 m),

and larger for big horses) is convenient—and essential for some horses who need stabling in bad weather. At home you will need a dry and secure place for your tack, equipment, hay, bedding, and feed.

Few horses like being kept on their own. If you cannot afford to buy another companion pony, why not consider having a retired one on loan—many people are glad to find good homes for their old friends, as are rescue charities. If you cannot afford to feed and care for another equine, consider a sheep or goat—but you'll need adequate fencing to keep it enclosed securely.

Many horse owners keep their animals at stables. There are several types to choose from:

ABOVE Although a horse is in its prime of life between the ages of seven and 12, a novice owner should not discount buying an older animal—even one in its mid to late teens. A well-schooled veteran is worth its weight in gold—if you can find one.

- **Owner responsible:** You rent a stable and pasture (or just pasture) on a weekly basis and are responsible yourself for feeding and caring for the horse on a daily basis.
- **Full-care:** You pay a fee each week for the owners to look after your horse for you, and exercise it when required. You simply go and ride it.
- **Part-care:** The stable owners look after your horse and feed it on a daily basis, but you groom and ride it. Some stables have different perceptions of the meaning of part-care, so ask.
- **Work-for-hire stable:** As for full-care but the stable uses your horse to teach clients in return for a reduced boarding charge. Again there are different perceptions of this type of boarding, so you must check.

Whatever type of boarding you choose, ensure that the stables are competently run and that your horse will, therefore, be well taken care of. Check also the quality of pasture, security of fencing, and the safety and suitability of stabling.

Whether you keep your horse at home or at a boarding stable, you will need access to off-road riding so bear this in mind.

FARRIER

It is essential that you find a farrier, the person who puts horseshoes on horses, who can accommodate you before buying a horse, otherwise you'll be stuck—"no foot, no horse!"

To find a registered, qualified, and competent farrier in your area, ask at your local boarding stable, riding school, and among your horse-owning acquaintances if they can recommend a farrier. Alternatively, contact the relevant farriers association that covers where you live (see Useful Addresses on pages 126–7).

VETERINARIAN

A veterinarian who is experienced in dealing with horses is essential. Ask at local stables, riding schools, and among your horse-owning acquaintances if they can recommend one.

FEED AND BEDDING

You must have dry space available to store feed and bedding, otherwise it will spoil. Feed should be kept in metal bins with secure lids so that vermin cannot eat and contaminate it. Hay and straw should be stored off the ground (on pallets, for example) to allow air to circulate under it and prevent rising damp.

Again ask local riding schools, boarding stables, and horse-owning acquaintances if they can recommend a good feed and hay merchant.

TRANSPORT

Once you've found a horse to buy you'll need to get it home. Some vendors will arrange this for you at an agreed cost. Otherwise you'll have to arrange it yourself. Local riding schools and boarding stables sometimes provide a transport service, so ask. If they don't they can often recommend a service. Many transporters insist that any equines they carry have up-to-date vaccinations to avoid spreading disease, so check that the horse you are thinking of buying complies with this requirement.

To travel safely, the van or trailer must be in sound, roadworthy condition, and the horse must be adequately protected against bumps and scrapes with boots, a poll guard, and a tail guard. Depending on the weather, it may need a blanket also. If this equipment is not supplied with the animal and the transporter cannot lend it to you, you will have to buy it before getting the horse—so ensure you ask the vendor what sizes to purchase. Don't forget you

will also need a halter (headcollar) and lead rope to tie the horse up when it travels.

RIDING AND PONY CLUBS, AND LOCAL EQUESTRIAN GROUPS

While you do not have to join a local riding club, doing so can provide a source of equestrian entertainment, socializing, activities, and new friends. Clubs often arrange shows and events you can take part in. To find your nearest club, ask at local stables and riding schools, and also see Useful Addresses on pages 126–7.

INSTRUCTION

It is helpful to carry on with riding lessons even when you own your own horse. In some cases having lessons is the only way to help you overcome problems with your horse. Some instructors will come to you, providing you have a suitable area to school in, and others you will have to travel to. If neither option is available to you, then you'll have to travel without your horse to a riding school for lessons in honing your riding and handling techniques.

FINDING A SUITABLE HORSE

Your first step in finding the perfect equine partner is to ask horsy acquaintances and your riding instructor if they know of any suitable horses for sale. Good animals are generally sold by word of mouth rather than by advertisement.

There is an old saying, *caveat emptor*, which means "buyer beware," and this is true of

ABOVE LEFT AND RIGHT
When looking at a horse or pony to purchase, think carefully about whether it will suit your physical conformation, temperament, and level of competence.

buying a horse. What may appear to be a perfect mount when you see and try it at the vendor's premises, may prove totally unsuitable once you take it home and get to know one another properly. Few sellers will allow you to take animals on trial so you really don't have a lot of opportunity to discover the animal's traits and habits before you buy it. This is why it is such a wise move to take your instructor with you when you see and try potential purchases.

Do not discount older horses; an aged (and "forgiving") school horse can give an inexperienced and novice owner years of wonderful, confidence-building service, whereas a novice youngster may prove far too much for that person's level of experience and knowledge.

How and where you will keep the animal determines the type of horse you should buy. If you intend it to live outdoors permanently always bear the climate in mind. A tougher "native" type will be more suited to an outdoor life than a thin-skinned Thoroughbred.

Your own build and temperament play an important role in deciding on a horse. If you are not terribly confident, then you do not need a flighty and nervous animal; a heavy rider needs an animal up to weight, while a small and light rider may have trouble controlling a tall, strong horse and shouldn't get such a horse. Choose a size and type on which you feel comfortable and safe. Whether you choose a mare, gelding, or stallion is up to you. Boarding stables willing to take stallions, however, are few and far between, plus they need experienced care and handling so are not ideal first horses for novice owners. Mares can be temperamental during their periods of estrus, some

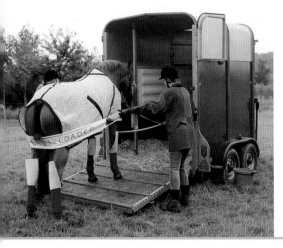

BELOW Loading a horse into a van.

more so than others. Geldings are considered to be more even-tempered, but this isn't always the case. Color is a personal choice. However be aware that gray horses tend to be prone to melanoma (abnormal tissue growths that can be either benign or malignant), which can be seen under the tail, under the gullet, on the face, and where glands are close to the skin's surface. If tumors can be seen on the outside of the horse, there may be more hidden away inside.

Always ask the owner why the horse is for sale to try to ascertain whether it is for a genuine reason, or because there is a problem with the animal. If the horse is freezemarked (see glossary, page 124), ask to see its identification papers to check that it is not stolen. Check also that any relevant breed and vaccination certificates are in order.

When trying the horse, follow these guidelines:

- First ask the owner to ride it in all paces, over jumps, and in traffic. Watch how the rider applies aids and how the horse reacts to them. If you buy the animal without knowing how best to ride it and then apply aids that it doesn't understand, you will start off with a problem. If the animal misbehaves with its owner, be wary: it may be that the owner is a terrible and unsympathetic rider, or that the horse may need reschooling.
- Find out if the seller actually runs the horse or is an agent.
- Check what state the facilities are in.
- Ask to see the horse loaded into a van or trailer if possible.
- See it ridden in company and by itself.
- See how easily it is caught in the field, and how it reacts to being tacked up and groomed. Does it object to being tied up?

- Is the horse friendly and interested in what is going on around it?

- Does it appear to be in good condition, healthy, and its feet well cared for? A sick horse will look listless, have a dull coat, may have mucus in its eyes and nostrils, and may cough or wheeze.

- Is it wormed and vaccinated up to date? Ask to see certificates if they are available— efficient owners will have records on hand.

- Is it easy to shoe? Ask who shoes it and for a contact number so you can check.

- Ask how the horse is kept (stabled or turned out) and what it is fed and how much. You need to know this if you buy the animal because diet changes can severely upset the digestive system.

- Does the horse have any vices, such as weaving, crib-biting, kicking, biting, head shaking, and so on? If its stall and door are chewed or kicked to bits, then beware!

- Is the horse happy in a stall? Some hate being confined and this can be a problem if you ever need to stable it.

- Always ask about the horse's likes, dislikes, and foibles. You need to know these so that you are aware of them and are prepared, or so that you don't change its daily riding care and routines too much.

PRE-PURCHASE VETTING

To assure yourself that the animal you intend on purchasing is physically healthy, it is a good idea to have a veterinarian examine it first. In a basic examination, the veterinarian will test its heart, breathing, eyesight, hearing, general condition, and check its age (as far as he or she is able, because aging equines becomes more difficult as they get older). He or she will also advise whether or not the animal is suitable for

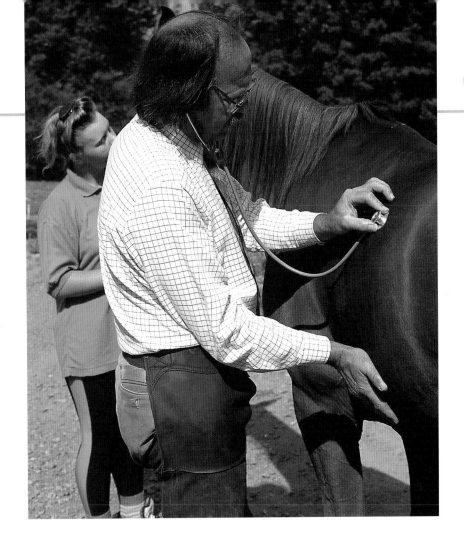

the activities you intend to do with it. It is also a good idea to ask the veterinarian to do a blood test to check for painkillers and sedatives (both of which can be used by unscrupulous vendors to mask a horse's unsoundness or behavior problems), and a test that will determine whether or not the horse suffers from a high worm infestation that can cause severe problems later on.

Obviously a veterinarian cannot see inside a horse, its joints, and its feet, and may therefore not be able to diagnose problems hidden from view without doing a more detailed examination, which involves X-rays, various blood tests, and other technical observations. This would entail getting the animal, if the vendor agreed to it, to an equine hospital—and more expense for you.

Never accept a veterinarian certificate from the vendor. Beware if the vendor won't agree to the horse being examined by a veterinarian of

ABOVE Having the horse vetted before purchase is a wise precaution.

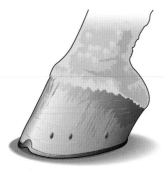

ABOVE A well-shod foot.

your choice prior to purchase. Having a horse vetted before buying is expensive, but worth it if it prevents you from purchasing something that is unsound, ill, or totally unsuitable. Include vetting in your horse purchase budget.

Finally, never buy on impulse. Go through the pre-purchasing paces carefully, and, if possible, sleep on it. Owning a horse is an enormous commitment.

INSURANCE

If your horse becomes sick and requires veterinary attention, this can be expensive— even running into several thousand dollars. So for peace of mind you can insure your horse against these fees. Perhaps more importantly, it's a good idea to insure you and your horse against a third-party claim in the event of damage to property or an accident caused by your horse. There are some insurance companies that specialize in equestrian policies, and it pays to shop around for the best deal to suit you. Ask your veterinarian for advice when choosing a company—they have experience of which companies deal fairly and quickly with claims, and which do not. You may also wish to insure yourself against injury, so again shop around for the best possible coverage. Sometimes being a member of an equestrian association automatically insures you against third-party claims, so it's worth investigating this.

Regarding tack and equipment, if you have a household insurance policy any riding equipment you own may be covered by that in certain circumstances, so it can save you money if you check this before taking out a fresh one. Always take the time and trouble to read your policy carefully before agreeing to it— especially the small print—to ensure you are

covered for everything you want to be, or think you are. If you are unsure about anything on an insurance policy—terms and conditions, and so on—contact the company concerned and ask them to explain it in a way you can understand. Always make a note of any correspondence with insurance companies—the conversation, the date, time, and who you spoke to—for future reference in case of a claim.

HORSE CARE

ON GRASS

Ideally, to remain happy and healthy as nature intended, horses should live out in fields where they have access to good pasture—they graze for around 18 hours per day in order to ingest enough nutrients from grass—and have the freedom to play and relax. A form of shelter is necessary, as mentioned earlier, as is access to a plentiful supply of clean water (horses drink about six to 12 gallons (22 to 45 liters) per day

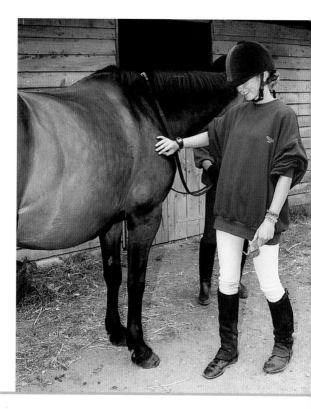

depending on their size and the weather). Water buckets or troughs should be cleaned at least once a week, and more often in warm weather, to remove dirt, slime, and algae. If you have freezing weather, break the ice as often as you can daily so your horse can drink. If you use an old bath to contain water, ensure the taps are removed because they can cause injuries. Remove manure from fields at least once a week, daily if possible because this makes the job quicker and easier, to help maintain sweet grazing and keep down parasite infestation.

When living outdoors, horses should be checked at least twice daily to ensure they are in good health and have suffered no injuries. Pick their feet out too and check for loose shoes. Walk around the boundary fencing also to ensure it is sound, and check the field for potential hazards and poisonous plants. Horses and ponies that are allowed to get overweight on good grazing (due to enforced rest through injury or under-exercise) are at risk from

laminitis, an extremely painful and potentially life-threatening foot ailment. Gorging on young, spring grass is a major trigger for this ailment, but stabled horses on too rich a diet for their work requirements are also in danger of contracting this condition.

Horses that live on good pasture do not need supplementary feeding in the growing seasons, unless they are worked extremely hard or the weather is so dry that there isn't much grass to eat. However, during winter they will need good quality hay, and some horses—the old, young, and those in regular daily work—will require hard feed too, to maintain body condition and health.

STABLED

Keeping a horse confined is unnatural, therefore every effort must be made to ensure it is turned out for several hours every day to play, stretch its legs, and relax fully. A stabled horse needs regular daily exercise to prevent it from

PICKING OUT THE FEET

No matter how bombproof and quiet you think the horse is, always ensure it is aware of your presence before moving toward its hindquarters—move from its front to back, never directly to its rear. Always ensure the horse is securely tied up. Use a hoofpick from heel to toe to clean out the feet, not toe to heel when it might get caught in the frog. Check for nails and other foreign objects that may have become lodged in the feet. Also observe the state of the shoes and clenches. Feet should be checked and cleaned out at least twice daily, and before and after rides.

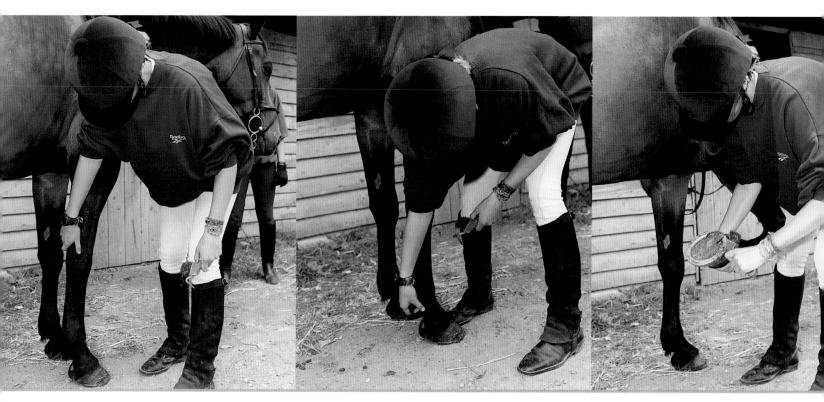

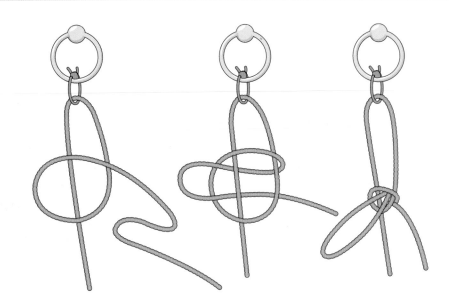

QUICK RELEASE KNOT

Tying up a horse or a haynet should always be done with a quick-release knot, to enable it to be released quickly and easily in an emergency. Never tie a horse's lead rope directly to a fixed point; tie a piece of baling string (single-stranded only, not doubled and preferably not the nylon variety because this is hard to snap) to the fixed point first and then attach the lead rope to the string. This is done so that the string, not the horse's neck, will break in an emergency. Haynets should be tied up high enough so that horses will not get their legs caught in them. When tying them up, allow for when they are empty (when they will hang down lower).

becoming bored, and to maintain fitness, health, and condition. It should have constant access to good-quality hay to eat, supplementary feeds (if necessary depending on the work it does) given at regular times, a plentiful supply of fresh, clean water, and a suitable "bed" to stand on.

There are many different types of bedding available, depending on where you live. There is straw (oat, barley, or wheat, with the latter being the most suitable), clean softwood shavings, peat, sand, earth, rubber matting, and shredded paper. Beds should be deep enough to prevent the horse from lying directly on concrete floors, and wet patches and manure must be removed daily. Building the bed up around the sides of the stable will help prevent drafts and stop the horse getting cast (when the horse rolls over and gets its legs stuck against the wall of its stall).

Feed and water buckets should be kept scrupulously clean, with water being changed twice a day and buckets scrubbed out to prevent a build-up of slime and algae (use plain water or a saline solution to do this, never use soap, and rinse well after scrubbing). Hay can

be fed in racks fixed to the wall, in small-holed hay nets, or from the floor. The latter is generally safer, although you will have more wastage. Racks take up valuable space, while hay nets have a nasty habit of coming unattached and getting tangled up in horses' feet.

Stalls and barns should be well ventilated, but not drafty, and doors should always open outward. Never padlock stable doors in case you need to get a horse out quickly in an emergency. Do not shut top doors except in extremely bad weather conditions. Windows, whether glass or plastic, should be barred to prevent a horse accidentally putting its head through them.

Two methods of tying up a haynet.

FEEDING

Equine digestive systems are designed to eat little and often. Living unrestricted in the wild, horses travel around to select the natural herbage (grasses, shrubs, trees, and herbs) they need to eat in order to maintain good condition and health. The availability and nutritional content of herbage depends on the season; in growing seasons, horses eat well, their bodies storing fat for seasons when food is scarcer and is not as nutritious. Living in captivity, a horse's diet is restricted to whatever pasture, dried grass, such as hay or haylage (known as bulk feed), and concentrates (supplementary cereal feeds) its owner provides.

Pasture should contain a good selection of leafy and nutritious grasses; rye, timothy, cocksfoot (American orchard), clover, alfalfa, sweet vernal, and meadow fescue are all good grasses for horses. However it is said that fescue can cause problems in pregnant mares, such as thickening of the placenta and spontaneous abortion. Hay should be light green-brown in appearance and smell sweet (rather like loose tea), be crisp and dust-free. It should contain lots of different good grasses and seed heads. Do not feed moldy, dusty, or rank-smelling hay. The simplest solution to feeding cereals is to give ready-made pony pellets or mixes. These are nutritionally balanced and contain essential minerals and vitamins. Although you can feed them dry, I prefer to dampen mixes or pellets slightly before feeding to make them easier to chew and swallow. To provide your horse with extra bulk feed (essential for the smooth operation of the digestive system), add chaff (chopped hay, or barley or oat straw) or well-soaked sugar beet nuts or shreds. Never feed dry sugar beet because it will swell inside the horse and cause severe colic. Remember, always read feeding instructions on the bags first and don't hesitate to consult your veterinarian.

Depending on the type of work your horse does, you can buy different nuts or mixes for different required energy levels. A non-heating nut or mix is suitable for equines in light work, while racehorse and performance feeds are suitable for performance horses. It is said that horses can become bored with pellets or mixes, but I have never found this to be the case. Working out your horse's daily feed requirements is quite easy. Calculate your

BELOW Check that a horse's bed is thick and deep enough by pushing a stable fork down into it. If the fork strikes the floor the bed is too thin. Thick beds help prevent injury to the horse, shield it from drafts, encourage it to stale and not retain urine, and enable it to lie down and rest. Thin beds indicate an ignorant, uncaring, or a miserly owner.

horse's weight (using a weight tape, available from tack stores). The total daily feed requirement (dry weight) will be approximately 2.5 percent of its body weight. For example, the daily amount of food required per day by a 14hh pony weighing 880lb (400kg) would be: 880 x 2.5 divided by 100 = 22lb (10kg).

- A resting horse needs maintenance feed. This can consist of 100 percent grass or good quality hay (bulk feed).
- A horse in light work needs approximately 0 to 15 percent concentrates and 85 to100 percent bulk feed.
- A horse in medium work requires approximately 15 to 30 percent concentrates and 85 to 70 percent bulk feed.
- A horse in hard work requires approximately 30 to 45 percent concentrates and 70 to 55 percent bulk feed.

The ratio of bulk to concentrate can be altered depending on how your horse fares. Some will need more bulk and less concentrates than others to maintain condition and energy for work, depending on the time of year.

Because your horse's stomach is small in relation to the animal's size, do not present it with a huge bucketful of feed to eat all in one go. If you do this a digestive upset may occur. Give its daily concentrate ration in several small feeds (morning, mid-afternoon, and night, for example). Each feed should comprise no more than 4½lb (2kg) dry weight.

Do not make sudden changes in diet; instead do it gradually to avoid digestive disturbance. Always try to feed at the same time every day—horses get anxious and upset when their feedtimes are altered. Keep feed buckets and utensils scrupulously clean. Some horses become overly energetic or excitable on "sweet"

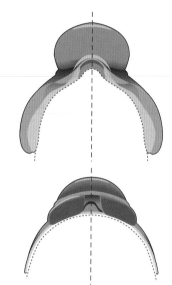

ABOVE A correctly fitting saddle.

BELOW Ill-fitting saddles may cause the horse great discomfort, and injury. From top to bottom; too narrow; twisted; unevenly stuffed.

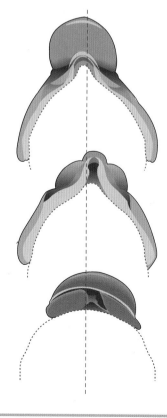

feeds (i.e. those with added molasses), so if this is the case with yours, buy non-molassed feeds.

Finally, avoid riding your horse for about an hour after supplementary feeding. Riding it on a full stomach can cause colic.

TACK

SADDLE AND BRIDLE

A new saddle and bridle will cost several hundred dollars, but you can often find good-quality secondhand ones at bargain prices. However, inexperienced horse owners are advised to buy their tack from a reputable saddler, who will come and correctly fit your horse for a saddle and bridle (whether new or secondhand). Ill-fitting tack causes great discomfort and pain to a horse, while unsafe tack presents an injury risk to both horse and rider. Even if your new horse comes complete with its tack, it does not mean that the tack is safe or fits the animal correctly and comfortably, so get an experienced person (your instructor or a saddler) to check it out for you.

Tack should be cleaned at least once a week, more if it gets really dirty, and preferably after each time you use it. Use a quality brand of saddle soap, and leather oil to soften and preserve new or dry leather. Bits need washing with clean water after every use. Never use soap on bits; your horse will not appreciate the taste. Be vigilant in keeping girths, and saddle pads if used, free from grease build-up, dirt, and hair, otherwise rubbing will occur. Check stitching each time you clean tack to ensure it is sound and safe—especially on stirrup leathers, girths, and around buckles. Check the girth strap fixings too because these have a lot of strain put on them.

BLANKETS

Depending on the type of horse you have and where you live, it may need a blanket to protect it from wet and cold weather. However, many equines do not need or welcome blanketing, providing they have sufficient food, shelter, and are in good condition. A horse will definitely need blankets if it is thin-skinned or clipped during cold and wet weather. If a horse is clipped at this time, it will need blankets to replace its heavy winter coat. Horses are clipped so they are easier to groom when in work; however, they can work just as well with a winter coat providing they receive adequate care and attention. It takes a bit more time and effort to groom, because a horse with a thick coat worked hard will sweat more, but the horse is better off with its natural coat than without it.

Stable blankets are designed for use in a stable, while New Zealand rugs and turn-out blankets are designed for outdoor use. It's advisable to have two of each so that if one gets wet through or damaged, you have a spare available. There are many different designs and weights of blanket available, so ask your instructor or saddler for help and advice in choosing one. Blankets are measured in feet and inches and to ascertain the correct size for your horse, measure your horse from the center of its chest, under the belly to the furthest point of its hindquarters.

The best blankets to use are those with cross surcingles that help ensure that no pressure is put on the horse's spine. Well-fitting blankets should not slip—if they do they will not provide proper protection and will cause great discomfort. Neither should a blanket rub at the shoulders, nor press down on the withers. To check for this, slip your hand under the rug at this point and see what pressure, if any, it puts on your hand. Rug linings should be kept clean and free from hair build-up, which causes rubbing and irritation. Brush them off daily.

BELOW LEFT A well-fitted stable rug.

BELOW RIGHT A well-fitted New Zealand rug.

GROOMING

A BASIC GROOMING KIT

- Dandy-brush: This has widely spaced, stiff bristles to remove loose hair and dry mud.
- Body brush: This has soft, densely packed, short bristles to provide deep coat cleansing and to groom sensitive areas such as the head as well as the mane and tail.
- Hoof pick: Essential for cleaning out feet.
- Water brush, comb, or vented mane-and-tail brush: Similar to a dandy-brush, it has softer bristles, and is used to groom manes and tails, and clean muddy feet.
- Soft cotton cloth or old towel: Use this for a final coat polish.
- Two sponges: The first is for the eyes and nose, and the other is for the dock and sheath/udder. Use different colors so you don't get them mixed up.
- Metal curry comb: This is used to clean out the body brush.

Regular grooming helps keep a horse clean and healthy. When grooming, use the hand nearest the horse; you'll be able to put more weight behind it and do a more effective job. Take care not to press too hard on ticklish or sensitive horses. Some horses prefer cactus cloths to brushes. When using a body brush, clean it out with the curry comb every couple of strokes. Horses generally like being groomed, and grooming helps build a close relationship between horse and owner. However, field-kept horses need to retain their natural coat oils in order to protect their skin in wet weather, so avoid bathing and over-grooming—simply brush off dried-on dirt and dandruff to make your horse presentable if riding, paying particular attention to where saddlery fits. Wet mud should be left to dry before being brushed off.

Only bath your horse (using equine shampoo) in warm weather, otherwise it may get a chill. Always rinse shampoo out from the coat very thoroughly or skin irritation and a dull coat may result. Horses often appreciate

ABOVE Grooming a horse is an important part of socializing with it, and checking its condition on a regular basis, as well as helping to keep it clean and healthy.

sweaty areas being washed down with clean water after exercise, but never leave a wet horse (from bathing or sweating) to dry in direct sunlight because scalding may occur.

The feet should be picked out and cleaned daily, before and after rides. Check for loose shoes, risen clenches, and foreign objects embedded in the foot. Neglected feet give rise to lameness and diseases such as thrush (a fungal condition affecting the frog clefts). Clean your horse's eyes, nose, and dock daily. Male horses' sheaths and mares' udders should be cleaned at least once a week to prevent a build-up of smegma or wax. While grooming, take the opportunity to check the body for signs of injury, and also coat parasites such as lice and ticks.

ROUTINE TREATMENTS

VACCINATION

All horses should be immunized against tetanus, a fatal condition for which there is no cure once an animal contracts it. Tetanus spores live in the soil and enter the bloodstream through cuts and grazes. Once immunized, yearly boosters are required. Other ailments you should consider are equine influenza, encephalomyletis, leptospirosis, strangles, rhinopneumonitis, and rabies. Some horses react to vaccines, so be aware that this may happen. Your veterinarian has to administer immunizations and fill in the relevant certificate. If boosters lapse, then the animal will have to have a full course of immunizations again. In the United States, statutory requirements vary from state to state, so check with your veterinarian to find out what is necessary in your area. Many shows and events insist upon entered horses having up-to-date

immunization certificates, thereby helping to prevent the spread of disease.

WORMING

Equines need regular worming treatment to prevent internal parasites from causing gut damage and poor health. Failure to worm your horse properly may result in ailments such as colic, a failure to thrive, or death.

You can buy worming treatments (in paste, powder, gel, or granule form) from licensed equestrian stores, pharmacies, and veterinarians. Your veterinarian will advise on a suitable worming program for your horse.

TEETH RASPING

Your horse's mouth and teeth should be checked at least once a year by a veterinarian or reputable equine dentist (your veterinarian may be able to recommend one). Old and young horses should have their mouths and teeth checked twice a year. Sometimes teeth are worn unevenly causing sharp edges, which can result in mouth damage, pain on eating, and discomfort when the bit is in place.

If your horse shows unusual signs that could indicate mouth discomfort, such as head shaking, increased salivating, resistance to the bit, or it isn't eating properly, then get your veterinarian to check it. Sometimes foreign objects, taken into the mouth while grazing or eating hay or even splinters from stable or fence chewing, become lodged in the mouth.

MINOR AILMENTS

Once you get to know your new horse you'll be able to identify its signs of good health and when it appears to be sick. A healthy horse appears happy, contented, in good condition, has a glossy coat, and urinates and defecates normally. A sick horse may be depressed and miserable, appear "tucked up," is cold, shivery, may be rolling abnormally, and not urinating or defecating normally.

Your horse's vital signs (VS) are its temperature, pulse rate (PR), and respiration rate (RR). These should be taken when the animal is at rest, and the best way of learning how to take them is to get your veterinarian or instructor to show you. Vital signs can change depending on the weather, level of fitness and heart rate, so when you get a new horse make a note of its VS on a daily basis over a period of weeks, in both warm and cold weather, to ascertain an average of what's normal for that animal.

- **Temperature: 100.5°F is normal, but it can vary slightly. Your veterinarian should be called if your horse's temperature drops below 100°F or rises above 101.5°F.**
- **Pulse rate: 35-40 heart beats per minute at rest is normal (a large animal's PR is lower than a small one's).**
- **Respiration rate: eight to 12 breaths per minute is normal, depending on the size of the animal. Big horses breathe at lower rates than small ones.**

If you are ever unsure about your horse's health, call the veterinarian. Minor cuts and grazes to the body and legs can be treated easily by cleaning with saline solution and applying antiseptic ointment or powder, but more serious injuries should be treated professionally. It's a wise idea to invest in a book on equine ailments (see Further Reading on page 127) so you can judge when to call the veterinarian and when you can treat your horse yourself.

SHOEING AND FOOT CARE

Ensuring your horse's feet are maintained in a sound, healthy condition is paramount to your horse's comfort and your continued riding enjoyment.

A horse's feet need trimming and checking every four to 12 weeks, depending on horn growth rate and general foot condition. If your horse only works on soft surfaces, such as grass or in an arena, it may not need shoes. Horses that are ridden on hard surfaces, such as roads and stony tracks, will almost certainly need shoes to protect their feet, and these will need resetting or replacing every four to eight weeks, depending on foot growth and shoe wear.

Farriers are busy people and always in demand, so book your farrier weeks in advance. Ideally, make the next appointment every time he or she attends your horse. Make sure you have your horse ready with clean feet and waiting on time for your farrier, on a hard surface and with well-lit shelter available in bad weather. Stay with your horse while its feet are seen to. Don't leave the farrier with it on his or her own in case it misbehaves. Always pay your farrier promptly—failure to do so may result in his or her refusal to shoe your horse in future which will leave it in dire straits.

BELOW Farriery is one of the horse owner's major expenses.

Equestrian activities and competing 12

LEFT For many riders, competing with their horses is their ultimate ambition. It's the taking part that counts, not the winning, so always remember to be a good sportsperson no matter what.

The beauty of horse riding is that there are many different kinds of equestrian activities—competitive and non-competitive—that you can continue to enjoy discovering. If you do not like jumping, then there are plenty of other equally exciting and rewarding disciplines in which to take part.

A BRIEF INTRODUCTION TO VARIOUS DISCIPLINES

The activities listed provide a brief introduction to various disciplines; more in-depth information can be found in equestrian books and specialist magazines pertaining to the activities you are particularly interested in. (See Further Reading on page 127.)

If classes or competitions are "affiliated" (to a particular discipline's official association or society), then you (and your horse) will need to be registered with that body in order to compete. Some shows insist upon the horse having an up-to-date vaccination certificate, or a height certificate. Your vet will advise on these matters.

CLASSICAL RIDING

Classical riding is a form of training that results in perfect harmony between horse and rider—as portrayed by the famous white Lipizzaner stallions and their riders of Vienna's Spanish Riding School. Basically, classical riding consists of the horse requiring its rider to guide it when to perform transitions, paces, and movements, and the rider requiring the horse to respond to his or her aids.

With advanced training, horse and rider will be able to perform "High School" dressage movements such as piaffe and passage. Any type of horse and rider can enjoy, and also become proficient at, classical riding with the correct training.

RIDING FOR THE PHYSICALLY DISADVANTAGED

Physically disadvantaged people can take part in and enjoy many of the equestrian disciplines listed, and there is no barrier to age or ability—nor horse-ownership. The key to the successful riding or driving of horses is to find and join a riding for the disabled group who will start you on the road to fun and success in the saddle. As well as being brilliant exercise in the fresh air, riding is a wonderfully social sport where you'll meet many new friends—equine and human alike.

BELOW Whatever the type or color of your horse or pony, there is a competition geared to suit.

LEFT Many people think dressage is an elitist equestrian activity, but in fact anyone can enjoy it. Dressage competitions cater to all levels, and dressage to music is great fun for horse and rider.

FAR LEFT A father taking part in a pony club competition.

DRESSAGE

Although "dressage" sounds complicated, and therefore intimidating, it isn't. All that dressage comprises is the ability to perform paces and school movements at set points in an arena in a correct and proper manner, with the horse obedient to the rider's commands. Marks are awarded for the correctness of the test movements done. There are competitions for all levels, from training levels upward, and most types of horse are suitable to begin with, although at advanced levels those of a light and athletic build are better equipped physically to perform certain movements.

DRIVING

Driving is an equestrian discipline enjoyed by people of all ages and horses of all types. You do not have to own a horse and carriage; there are driving centers where you can be taught how to drive. If you have your own horse and want to drive it, finding a good instructor is essential if you are to learn the skill involved in driving properly and safely. You can drive simply for your own pleasure around local roads, or you can compete. There are many different driving disciplines to take part in, from single pony to four-in-hand.

ENDURANCE RIDING

Endurance riding is the fastest-growing equestrian sport, with more and more riders discovering the pleasure and thrill of completing a ride over wonderful countryside in a set time with a sound horse. Endurance ride distances are between 20 and 100 miles (32 to 60 km), against the clock or at a set

speed. Also available are pleasure rides that are not competitive, and these range in length from five to 20 miles (8 to 32 km), with those completing gaining a rosette or certificate.

At lower levels of the sport, up to 50 miles (80 km), any sort of horse is suitable, providing it is sound and fit enough for the distance to be traveled, but at higher levels of speed and distance, Arab-type horses tend to be better equipped to cope. As you progress to rides of over 20 miles (32 km) you will need a "back-up crew"—friends or family members to help care for the horse and rider before, during, and after the ride.

Horses are vetted before and after rides to ensure they are healthy and sound. Failure to pass the inspection results in elimination (being "spun").

ABOVE Driving is a discipline enjoyed by all ages.

EVENTING (HORSE TRIALS)

Eventing comprises three disciplines—dressage, cross-country, and showjumping. Horse trials are run over one, two, or three days depending on the event's level of difficulty. At advanced three-day events there is also an endurance phase where the horse and rider have to negotiate a set distance of roads and tracks and jump a series of steeplechase fences. The marking system for eventing is based wholly on penalties —the rider with the least penalties wins. Competing in horse trials demands confident and skillful riding from the rider, and boldness and athletic ability from the horse. Horse trials are an all-around test of a horse and rider's ability. The dressage phase is designed to test the horse's obedience, the cross-country its boldness and jumping skill over fixed obstacles, while the showjumping phase tests the horse's fitness and obedience after the excitement and effort of the cross-country.

MOUNTED GAMES

Mounted games are tailored to the age and ability of both horse and rider. Although primarily a children's sport, some shows hold classes for adults too—after all, why should the kids have all the fun! Games are many and varied; they include pole-bending, sack races, egg-and-spoon races, trotting races, and stepping-stone dashes, to name but a few.

HORSEBALL

Any horse is suitable for playing horseball on, although if you want to compete at a high level you'll require a speedy and athletic mount. The object of this team sport is to score goals; the goal posts are situated at each end of the game arena. The ball is carried in a frame with a handle that the riders carry, passing it to other team members as they ride up the arena toward the goal, while the opposing team members try

ABOVE If you love the thrill of jumping a variety of obstacles at speed across country, then eventing is for you.

RIGHT Ponies tend to enjoy gymkhana games as much as their riders.

FAR RIGHT Anyone for polo?

their best to get possession of the ball and score their own goals.

If the ball is dropped the rider has to bend down and pick it up, so being balanced and supple is essential! A pick-up strap is attached to each stirrup iron, running under the horse's belly, to enable the rider to bend down and lean over as far as possible without falling out of the saddle. This is a physically demanding and close contact sport, and playing at advanced levels, though great fun, is not for the faint-hearted—horse or rider!

CROSS-COUNTRY

Cross-country involves riding over a course of field fences, usually within a set time limit. The height and difficulty of the obstacles vary, depending on the level of the competition, and other factors, such as the horse's height, and the rider's age and level of equestrian experience.

HUNTING

There are two types of hunting: blood sports and drag-hunting. In the former, a live quarry (fox, coyote, wild boar, or wild deer—depending on where you live) is chased through the countryside by specially trained hounds who are followed by riders on horseback. The quarry either escapes or is caught and killed instantly by the hounds or shot by the huntsman. While the object of the exercise is a traditional and effective form of pest control, riders who follow hounds generally do so for the thrill of riding across country and jumping the different natural obstacles in their path. It is also a useful form of training for potential event and jump-racehorses.

Drag-hunting does not entail the death of any quarry. First of all, a human "runner" lays a scent trail over a set course and distance, then specially trained hounds are released to follow that trail, followed by mounted riders. There are generally two or three trails laid, with a rest in between each. Drag-hunting is much faster than fox-hunting because time is not spent waiting around for hounds to find quarry, so boldness and confidence in galloping and jumping natural obstacles at speed is required from both horse and rider.

With both forms of hunting, there are generally gateways you can go through if you don't wish to jump fences, but this isn't always the case. To take part in fox-hunting or drag-hunting you need a horse that is obedient, won't kick hounds or other horses, and is stoppable when galloping in company.

ORIENTEERING

Particularly enjoyed in France where it is called Le Trec, mounted orienteering, is beginning to catch on as a thoroughly enjoyable equestrian sport that can appeal to riders of all ages and abilities. Basically, it involves showing a control of paces and negotiation of a small cross-country and obstacle course. Any type of horse is suitable and you don't need special equipment. You don't even need your own horse because some riding centers holding competitions will rent you a mount for the competition (providing you belong to a society whose membership includes insurance coverage).

POLO

Although viewed as an elitist sport, anyone can learn to play polo and it doesn't have to cost a

ABOVE If you have a young horse, showing in-hand is a good way of participating in competition as well as getting it used to different sights and sounds.

fortune. Initial lessons will be spent on a wooden horse, learning how to hold the mallet and hit the ball while at the same time maintaining a correct and secure position, before you are allowed to venture out onto the training ground on a safe and steady schoolmaster pony.

Played at low levels, you don't need a special polo pony—any horse will do. Horses generally love to take part. You can help improve your co-ordination and skill by "stick and balling" (hitting the ball accurately and aiming it in particular directions) at home, but always ensure your pony's legs are protected with boots.

POLOCROSSE

Polocrosse can be enjoyed by riders of all ages and abilities mounted on any type of horse, and is best described as a cross between polo and lacrosse on horseback. The object of this team sport is to score goals by scooping a ball up off the ground with a lacrosse-like stick incorporating a loose net, and passing it to other team members until one has a chance to shoot at the goal area.

As you become more proficient at picking up and passing the ball, the game becomes faster and faster, and can be quite physical as you make contact with opposing players. It's fantastic fun and the horses love it too.

This is a sport you can practice at home, and have great fun doing it.

SHOWING

There is a huge variety of showing classes available for all ages and abilities of horse and rider, both in-hand (where the rider leads the

horse) and ridden, so there is sure to be something for you and your horse to take part in.

Ridden classes are judged on the horse's type and suitability for particular categories (such as children's ponies, hunters, riding horses, and equitation, to name but a few). In-hand classes generally concentrate on a horse's breed or color, with marks awarded for type and perfection of color or markings.

Horse and rider presentation is important, with both having to be clean and equipped in the correct dress and tack to gain maximum points. In some ridden classes the judge rides competitors' horses, so it is important that the horse is well-mannered and amenable to being ridden by different people.

SHOWJUMPING

There are a variety of showjumping classes to suit different levels of ability of horse and rider, from small "clear round" courses, to those of Olympic proportions designed to test horse and rider to the limit. The idea is to complete a course of fences (which are designed to collapse if the horse touches them) without knocking them down or being penalized. Every time a fence is knocked down, the rider accrues four faults (penalties); a first refusal (when the horse won't jump) gains three faults, a second six faults, and three refusals leads to elimination; a fall of horse or rider gains eight faults. In classes against the clock, the idea is to complete a clear round in the fastest time possible.

SIDESADDLE

This elegant sport is open to females of all ages and abilities, and most types of horse are suitable, although cobby animals and those

FAR LEFT If you can maintain a good position and balance over small fences, then the higher ones will be a cinch.

LEFT You don't need to jump high fences or be terribly brave to have a go at novice showjumping. Many shows provide classes for first-timers, horses and riders alike.

with high or no withers can be difficult to fit with a sidesaddle. Finding an experienced instructor is essential if you want to learn the art of riding sidesaddle. As well as showing, other competitive sidesaddle activities include jumping and dressage.

VAULTING

Vaulting is a combination of riding, gymnastics, and dance. Basically the horse is fitted with a special vaulting pad with handles, and the rider sits on the pad like a saddle and performs a series of gymnastic-type exercises. The horse is on the lunge throughout and maintains a steady, slow canter.

Age is no barrier to vaulting, and you don't have to ride well to be good at it. The more you practice, the more agile and supple you become. It's great fun and excellent for building confidence, teaching feel, and learning to balance well on a horse. In fact, it is a super way of introducing beginners to riding horses. The only equipment you need is a schooling helmet, gymnastic shoes, leggings or sweatpants, and a close-fitting stretch top.

FAR LEFT Sidesaddle riding is both challenging and elegant. Competitions include showing, dressage, and jumping.

LEFT "Gymnastics on horseback"—vaulting is becoming more and more popular and you don't need to ride well to enjoy and be good at it.

LEFT Western riding is hugely popular throughout the world and there is a variety of classes to take part in.

WESTERN RIDING

Western riding is popular with all rider age groups because of its relaxed style and extremely comfortable saddle. Most types of horses are suitable and you don't need any special tack at the start. Emphasis is on teaching the horse to respond to the lightest of aids (called "cues" in Western riding), especially the voice. Contact with the mouth is minimal, with the rider's weight and legs, along with rein pressure on the horse's neck, being all that is required to direct a fully trained horse.

There are many competitive activities for Western riders to enjoy including barrel racing, pole bending, equitation, showing, reining, and trail classes. It's great fun!

RIDING AND PONY CLUBS

Joining a riding or pony club is a great way of making new friends, improving your riding ability and equestrian knowledge, and having the opportunity to compete. You will also be able to participate in club-organized outings to watch big shows, and lectures and demonstrations put on by well-known riders. There might even be camping vacations to go on. You don't have to have a horse to join a club, although it helps with riding activities; you may be lucky enough to be loaned a pony so you can participate.

BELOW Join a riding or pony club—you can't beat being part of a team.

EQUESTRIAN VACATIONS

Whatever your favorite equestrian activity, there is sure to be an equestrian vacation that caters to it. Or why not try your hand at a completely new discipline? Many equestrian magazines carry advertisements for a tempting selection of equestrian-oriented vacations. Tourism offices can also provide details of suitable establishments in their areas. And some holiday companies even cater to those people who wish to take their own horses on vacation with them to share a wonderful experience of riding in a different part of the country.

Whatever you choose, follow these guidelines:

- Check that establishments are licensed and insured.
- To gain maximum enjoyment from your vacation, be honest when informing the equestrian center of your riding ability.
- Read brochures carefully to check that what is offered by the center is what you want and expect. Get personal recommendations if possible.

ACTIVITIES FOR NON-HORSE OWNERS

There are many activities and hobbies a non-horse-owner can enjoy, with many costing very little. A selection of things to do includes:

- Attend local shows as a spectator.
- Collect equine memorabilia, such as postcards, horseshoes, books, and videos, horse brasses, ornaments, and so on.
- Adopt a horse, pony, donkey, or mule through a charity. In return for a small annual fee you will receive a photo of your adopted equine, plus regular updates on its progress. Plus you may have opportunities to go and see it.
- Consider sharing a horse. Some people cannot afford the money or time to keep and care for a horse by themselves so advertise for another person to help share the cost or time.
- Borrow equestrian books and videos from libraries—both are a good way of increasing your knowledge.
- Take out subscriptions to equestrian magazines in order to keep updated on developments in the horse world, as well as improve your riding and stable management knowledge (see Further Reading on page 127).
- Offer to work in return for riding privileges at local stables, riding schools, and for private owners.
- Help out at riding for disabled groups, where willing helpers are always needed, and also at local shows and clubs. Who knows what opportunities could arise by doing this.

ABOVE LEFT Going on a horse-riding vacation is a great way to see different areas of a country and enjoy your favorite sport at the same time.

ABOVE Why not have a day at the beach? If you have the transport and live near enough, head for the coast. Check with the relevant authority and Coast Guard first though to ensure it is permissible and safe. Some riding schools and boarding stables organize beach rides for those who haven't got their own horses.

To enjoy riding from the outset requires an enthusiasm for the sport and a good instructor. No matter what level you wish to achieve, your instructor should always make you feel special. To obtain satisfaction from riding, whether you want to just ride for pleasure or compete for your country at the Olympics, you need to feel confident and safe. To obtain both you have to have belief in yourself and your teacher.

Conclusion

I cannot emphasize strongly enough the importance of gaining effective instruction. First-class instruction will allow your seed of love for horses and interest in handling and riding them to ripen into a full-blown passion for this sport. As I have intimated previously, an instructor will either seduce or sour your desire to be part of and enjoy the world of the horse.

Many riders find contact with equines and riding a great stress-reliever; sometimes animals are far more willing and receptive to your emotions than humans can be. Whatever your particular need, never allow your own requirements to get in the way of the admiration, love, and respect you should always have for the horse, in whatever shape or form it presents itself. It may be miserable if you treat it badly, but it will never blame you. A horse's innocence and trust is complete; when you are with one you are enjoying something extremely precious. Never forget that. You are privileged indeed to communicate with it and therefore share some small part of its special world.

At one time animals were thought to be incapable of feeling emotions and sensations—pain, fear, thought, enjoyment, humor, sadness, love, hate, desire, indifference, and so on—as humans do. Thankfully those who truly love and appreciate animals, horses included, are disproving ignorant theories now. Their contributions, and boldness in challenging the "old school," are a breath of fresh air and are pioneering the way in improving horse care and riding methods.

I hope that this book helps you in some way to become the rider you wish to be, enjoy the sport safely and confidently, and care for horses in a fair, proper, and sympathetic way.

The following poem, from a book entitled *Foxhunting for Ladies* by Mrs O'Donohue, and dated around 1880, is, truly, "A Horse's Petition To His Owner."

Going up hill, whip me not.

Going down hill, hurry me not.

On level road, spare me not.

Of hay and corn, rob me not.

Of pure water, stint me not.

Of fresh air, deprive me not.

To damp bed, subject me not.

With brush and sponge, neglect me not.

Home from grass, physic me not.

Tired and hot, wash me not.

Sick or cold, chill me not.

With bit and reins, jerk me not.

When you are vexed, strike me not.

When old and grey, despise me not.

When past my labour, work me not.

When sick and dying, leave me not.

And, when dead...

Forget me not.

Aged: Horses and ponies over the age of eight are said to be aged. This is because a horse's age can be estimated by its teeth reasonably accurately up to that age, but not afterward.

Balance: Otherwise known as equilibrium. Balance is achieved when a rider can remain stable on a horse in all paces and movements, independent of the hands. A mounted horse is said to be balanced when its weight and that of its rider are distributed equally over all four of its legs and it can move comfortably and freely.

Barging: When a horse pushes past its handler.

Bend: Equine body flexion from head to tail.

Body protector: A specially designed and padded vest designed to absorb shock in the event of a fall, worn by the rider. Different weights are available depending on the level of protection required and the body weight of the rider.

Bolt (bolting): Running away out of control; also, a horse that eats its food greedily and quickly is said to bolt its food.

Bombproof: A safe and reliable horse suitable for novice riders.

Bulk feed: Also known as roughage or forage feeds, this includes grass, hay, haylage, alfafa, bran, sugar beet, and chaff (chopped hay or straw). These are feedstuffs that are high in fiber, low in nutrients, and contain carbohydrates (sugars and starches). Fiber is an essential part of the horse's diet to maintain digestive efficiency. Horses are designed to eat virtually constantly; living wild, their diet consists of natural herbage that is low in nutrients, so they have to eat a lot of it in order to extract the necessary daily nutrient intake. If a horse goes without food for too long, its digestive system ceases to function properly, causing digestive upset. It is therefore necessary to provide plenty of bulk feed daily (from grass, supplementary feedstuffs, or a combination of both depending on the season, amount of work the animal does, and how it is kept). Bulk feed normally makes up two-thirds of the daily ration for the average riding horse. The harder the horse works, the more nutrient- and protein-rich feed it needs to provide energy for work while still maintaining condition.

Cantle: Raised, curved part at the back of the saddle.

Cardiovascular fitness: Healthy heart and blood vessel operation, i.e. these organs are fit to cope with the exercise level required.

Cereals: These grain feeds are known as concentrated feedstuffs: oats, barley, corn, peas, beans, wheat products, and sorghum. They can be fed separately (known as straights), or bought in a ready-mixed and nutrient/forage balanced form (compound feeds), which is more convenient. They are high in carbohydrates, which produces energy for work—some cereals, such as oats, release this energy more quickly than others.

Chestnut: The horny growth (also known as castor) on the inside of a horse's leg (above the knee on forelegs and below the hocks on hindlegs).

Clear round: A jumping round completed without any faults or penalties.

Clenches (clinches): The visible part of a horseshoe nail that protrudes from the hoof wall. These should be bent down flat against the wall to hold the shoe secure on the foot. Clenches that have bent away from the hoof wall are known as risen clenches. The shoe will become looser the more clenches are risen.

Clipping: Shaving the coat off, wholly or partly.

Cob: A small, chunky, weight-carrying horse. Show cobs should not exceed 15.1hh.

Colic: Equine stomachache. Causes include digestive upset, internal parasites, twisted gut, gut infection, and poisoning. It varies in severity depending on the cause of the problem, and can be fatal. Veterinary attention should be sought immediately.

Company: Other equines (when turned out), or in the company of other horses and riders when riding out or schooling.

Concentrates: Cereal feedstuffs (also known as short or hard feed).

Condition: Condition describes the state of the horse's body. In "good condition" means it is healthy and it is carrying sufficient bodyweight (fat and muscle) in relation to the work it is doing. In "poor condition" means it is underweight. In "soft condition" denotes the animal is unfit for strenuous work, and this is generally a term used for an overweight horse turned out to pasture.

Conformation: A horse's shape, structure, and proportions to its size.

Contact: The "feel" between the horse's mouth and the rider's hands. The tension of the rein.

Cross-country: The equestrian sport that involves jumping fixed, natural-looking obstacles over a countryside course.

Cross surcingles: On horse blankets, these are the securing straps that cross over under the belly.

Dam: A horse's mother.

Dead to the leg: This describes a horse that does not respond to leg aids.

Diagonal: An angled line across a riding arena, as in a school movement to change the rein. Also, in trot, a horse's foreleg moving in unison with the opposite hindleg.

Discipline: Orderly self-control; also a type of equestrian sport, such as dressage or showjumping.

Dock: The bony part of a horse's tail. This term also describes the rectal area under the tail.

Dressage: The training of horses to be obedient to the rider's requests.

Electric fencing: Low-voltage electrified wire, nylon rope, or tape used to keep horses contained in a grazing area. Electrical shock impulses are supplied via an automobile battery or mains energizer that adapts voltage to a suitable level.

Equitation: The art of riding; horsemanship.

Estrus: The period when a female horse is fertile and receptive to mate with a male, usually five days every three weeks during spring and summer months. Also known as being "in season."

Filly: A female equine over one year and under four years old.

Fizzy: Of a horse, excitable, overly energetic.

Flexion: Bend; also when a horse relaxes (yields) its jaw to bit pressure and bends its head down (and sideways if required) at the poll.

Foal: A young equine under 12 months of age.

Forehand: A horse's front end, the head, neck, shoulders, and front legs—the part of the body that is in front of the saddle. "On the forehand" means that the horse is not using its hindquarters properly to produce impulsion.

Freezemark (freezebrand): An identifying mark, made by applying a freezing marker to a clipped area on the horse (usually the back or shoulder). This kills hair pigment cells, or the roots themselves in light-colored horses, resulting in a white-haired or bald mark. A brand.

Gelding: A male equine that has had its testicles removed, i.e. it has been castrated.

Give and take (contact): The rider's hands "give" when they relax contact pressure on the horse's mouth via the reins, and "take" when they apply pressure or contact on the mouth.

Gray: A dark-skinned horse with white hairs. An intermingling and pattern of black hairs denotes the type of gray (such as iron gray, dark gray, dapple gray, light gray). A white horse with pink skin is known as an albino. A cream-colored horse with pink skin is known as a cremello. Albinos and cremellos have blue-colored irises.

Ham-fisted: Heavy handed, i.e. rough and unyielding with the hands.

Hay: Dried grass used as a feedstuff. Meadow hay is cut from permanent pasture and contains a various mix of grasses and herbage, while seed hay is specially grown from specific grass seeds and, if tended properly, is usually of higher quality, being fairly weed-free.

Haylage: Grass that is cut and left to semi-wilt before being vacuum-packed and sealed in airtight plastic bales to preserve as much nutritional value as possible. It is dust-free, so ideal for horses with dust allergies or those prone to coughing when fed dry hay.

Horn: The tough, insensitive parts of the horse's foot, such as the hoof wall.

Impulsion: The forward and upward energy generated from the horse's hindlegs.

In-hand: Leading a horse as opposed to riding it.

Iris: The colored part of the eye.

Lateral (movement): Movement in which the horse makes ground both forward and sideways.

Leather oil: A blend of vegetable oils used to soften and preserve leather.

Livery yard: An establishment where equines are boarded.

Maintenance feed: Daily feed sufficient for a horse in light work or no work at all. Usually wholly bulk (hay or grass), or with added non-heating concentrates as necessary to supplement nutritional requirements in order to maintain adequate body condition.

Mare: A female equine over four years of age. Under that age it would be referred to as a filly.

Martingale: An item of tack designed to stop the horse throwing its head in the air beyond the point of control. Both a running martingale and a standing martingale are attached to the girth and pass through a neckstrap that holds the martingale in place, but the running martingale features two ring-ended leather straps which attach to each rein, while the standing martingale has just one strap that attaches to a cavesson noseband (and only a cavesson, as its action on dropped nosebands would be too severe).

Molting: Shedding hair.

Motorbike: A term used to describe a horse cutting across a corner with its inside shoulder leading, rather than bending correctly into it.

Mount: To get on a horse; also a term used to describe a ridden horse.

Mounting block: A stand, with steps, designed to make mounting a horse easier.

Neckstrap: A strap fastened, not tightly, around the base of a horse's neck to be used as a "safety handle" for a novice rider.

New Zealand rug: A waterproof and windproof outdoor horse blanket.

Non-heating: This is said of feedstuffs that are slow in releasing energy-giving carbohydrates. While oats and barley are similar in carbohydrate content, that in oats is released more quickly than in barley, hence the reason why oats have a reputation of "hotting up" horses.

Novelty classes: Fun show classes that most people can enter, such as "horse or pony that the judge would most like to take home," "fancy dress," and "most beautiful tail."

Over-horsed: A horse that is too big and/or strong for its rider to cope with.

Paces: Gaits, e.g., walk, trot, canter, and gallop.

Performance horses/ponies: Equines that are used for high-level, strenuous activities such as showjumping, eventing, endurance, and racing.

Pommel: Upward curving part of a saddle in front of the rider.

Pony mix (sweet feed): A ready-mixed, loose formulation of concentrate feeds containing added vitamins and minerals.

Pony pellets (nuts or cubes): A feed, similar to pony mix but in compressed pellet form.

Pupil: Of the eye, the round "black" opening in the eye through which light passes.

Quarters (hind): Comprises the rump (buttocks), pelvic area, and hindlegs.

Rhythm: Regularity of hoof beats and pace.

Roll (rolling): A circular motion; the term also describes when a horse lies down and rolls over, or tries to, from one side to the other.

Saddle soap: A special soap (in solid or liquid form) used to clean leather, composed mainly of glycerin (and sometimes other vegetable oils are added).

Saddlesore: Muscle soreness suffered after riding.

Schooling: Training a horse and/or rider.

Schoolmaster: A well-trained and obedient horse.

Scurf: Dirt and old skin flakes found in the coat.

Seat: The rider's bottom; the position in the saddle; and the part of the saddle between pommel and cantle on which the rider sits.

Shampoo (equine): A special, non-irritant, liquid soap used for washing horses.

Sheath: The open pouch of skin in front of the scrotum which houses a male horse's penis.

Shoes: Rims of steel nailed to horses' hooves, designed to protect the foot from becoming damaged and sore on hard and stony surfaces.

Sixth sense: An intuitive response or reaction that is not apparent to others.

Slipping the reins: Allowing the reins to slide freely through the fingers.

Smegma: The sebaceous secretion in a stallion's sheath.

Sorrel: A red-golden color varying in lightness (liver, dark, light red, chocolate), known as chestnut in the UK.

Sound(ness): A sound horse is one that has no physical ailment.

Spooked: Alarmed.

Spur: Metal gadgets attached to the heel of a rider's boot with a strap, designed to provide refined leg aids. They must never be used roughly, only stroked gently on the horse's side.

Stable blanket: A horse blanket that is designed for indoor use. Lining weights vary depending on the level of warmth required.

Stallion: An uncastrated male horse aged four years and over.

Stitch: A sharp, pricking, spasmodic pain in a rider's side, caused by muscle cramp.

Sugar beet: A by-product of sugar beet roots after the sugar content has been extracted. It may be bought in dry form in shreds, or cubes (nuts or pellets). It should always be soaked for 24 hours in cold water before feeding, because once wet it swells to twice its dry size. Always label the sugar beet feed bin prominently so it is not mistaken for pony nuts and fed dry by mistake. When soaked, sugar beet sours after a day or so, depending on the ambient temperature, so only soak the amount you are going to use the following day. When weighing sugar beet to feed, weigh the wet weight, not dry.

Supplementary feeding: This comprises any horse feed other than grass, such as hay and concentrates.

Tempo: Speed and rhythm, i.e. the measure of speed within the gait movements determining the distance covered per minute.

Tidbits: Treats given to horses as a reward, such as mint-flavored candies, apples, and carrots.

Transition: A change of pace, for example from walk to trot.

Trimming (dressing feet): Cutting and filing excess horn growth off the hooves to ensure the horse can move comfortably and level.

Turn-out blanket: A blanket designed to be worn outside by a horse to keep it dry and warm.

Udder: The organ that contains a female equine's mammary gland, which secretes milk for suckling foals via the udder's two teats.

Under-horsed: A rider is said to be under-horsed if his or her mount is too small for his or her size and weight.

Warm up: Light exercise that prepares the body for more strenuous activity.

Whip: A leather or synthetic material-covered stick, which can vary in length and type depending on the activity it is employed in, used to back up a rider's physical aids in admonishing or encouraging a horse.

Winding: When the breath is knocked from a rider's body, such as in a fall.

Work: Physical effort. Light work = body maintenance plus up to an hour's work per day that consists of mainly walking and trotting with little, if any, cantering; medium work = body maintenance plus up to 90 minutes work per day in all paces and jumping, plus competing at local level at weekends; hard work = body maintenance plus daily fitness training in all paces for competitive activities including racing, eventing, polo, endurance, hunting, and competing.

Yield: To "give," or relax pressure.

Listed federations and societies can be contacted to locate suitable riding schools and instructors, as well as other breed and discipline associations.

NORTH AMERICA

American Association for Horsemanship Safety
P.O. Box 39
Fentress, TX 78622
Tel (512) 488-2220
Fax (512) 488-2319
Riding instructor certification clinics; workshops on horsemanship and horse safety; Secure Seat riding clinics.

American Endurance Ride Conference
Suite 9, 11960 Heritage Oak
Auburn, CA USA 95603
Tel: (530) 823-2260
Fax (530) 823-7805
http://www.aerc.com

American Horse Shows Association
4047 Ironworks Parkway
Lexington, KY 40511
Tel (606) 258-2472
Fax (606) 231-6662
http://www.ahsa.org/

The American Horse Trials Foundation
3248 Paseo Gallita
San Clemente, CA 92672
Tel (949) 493-0198
Fax (949) 493-0269
E-mail <ahtf@juno.com>
Non-profit eventing association.

American Medical Equestrian Association
4715 Switzer Road
Frankfort, KY 40601
Tel/Fax (502) 695-8940
http://www.law.utexas.edu/dawson

American Riding Instructors Association
American Riding Instructor Certification Program

28801 Trenton Court
Bonita Springs, FL 34134
Tel (941) 948-3232
Fax (641) 948-5053
E-mail <aricp@aria.win.net>
Directory of ARICP Certified Riding Instructors.

Association of Riding Establishments of Ontario
76 - 7th Concession East
Milgrove, ON L0R 1V0
Tel (905) 689-0683
http://www.thetackbox.com/AREONT/

Brubacher Harness Shop
Box 6
6377 Main Street North
Wallenstein, ON N0B 2S0
Tel (519) 669 2064
Fax (519) 669-4422
brubhar@golden.net
Three-generation manufacturer and distributor of harnesses to Ontario's Mennonite community and to recreational and competitive carriage drivers.

Canadian Equestrian Foundation
Suite 200, 2460 Lancaster Road
Ottawa, ON K1B 4S5
Tel (613) 248-3433
Fax (613) 248-3484
http://www.equestrian.ca
The governing body for equestrian sport in Canada.

Canadian Livestock Records Corporation
2417 Holly Lane
Ottawa, ON K1V 0M7
Tel (613)731-7110
Fax (613)731-0704
http://www.clrc.on.ca
Maintains records on horse sales.

Canadian Ponies of the Americas Association
24281 - 65th Ave
Langley, BC V2Y 2H1
http://members.xoom.com/CPOA/poa

Canadian Pony Club
Box 4256, Station E
Ottawa, ON K1S 5B3
Toll-Free Tel 1-888-286-PONY
Fax (403) 230-PONY
http://www.ebtech.net/pony club

Canadian Pony Society
R.R. 1
Jarvis, ON N0A 1J0
Tel (905) 768-1252

Canadian School of Horseshoeing
R.R. 2
Guelph, ON N1H 6H8
Tel (519) 824-5484
http://www.horseshoes.com

Canadian Sport Horse Association
Box 98, 40 Elizabeth Street
Okotoks, AB T0L 1T0
Tel (403) 938-0887
Fax (403) 938-5441
http://www.canadian-sport-horse.org

Canadian Veterinary Medical Association
339 Booth Street
Ottawa, ON K1R 7K1
Tel (613) 236-1162
http://www.cvma-acmv.org
Website is a rich source of information.

Cavalier EPC Canada Inc.
649 Ontario Street
P.O.Box 10
Stratford, ON N5A 6S8
Tel (519)-273-3122
Fax (519)-273-4215
E-mail <kristins@cavalier.on.ca>
Canadian distributor of equestrian apparel, including Sweden's Mountain Horse.

Equestrian Products Corp.
360 Kiwanis Blvd
P.O. Box 159
Hazleton PA 18201
Toll-Free Tel 1-800-526-6987 Toll-Free Fax 1-800-778-1638

E-mail <mountainhorse@eisers.com>
U.S. distributor of equestrian apparel.

The Equine Research Centre
50 McGilvray Street
Guelph, ON N1G 2W1
Tel (519) 837-0061
Fax (519) 767-1081
http://www.erc.on.ca
Affiliated with the University of Guelph School of Veterinary Medicine.

Eventing Canada
59 Hillside Drive
Toronto, ON M4K 1M2
Tel/Fax (416) 429-1415
http://www.eventing.ca

Farrier & Hoofcare Resource Center
http://www.horseshoes.com
On-line source of farrier school listings and other information.

The Guild of Professional Farriers
P.O. Box 684
Locust, NC 28097
E-mail <theguild@horseshoes.com>

Heartland Publications
P.O. Box 600
Cedar Vale, KS 67024.
Fax (316) 758-2683
http://www.hlpub.com
Publisher of books on all things equine.

Horse Trials Canada
R.R. 1
Dwight, ON P0A 1H0
Tel (705) 635-1569

North American Riding for the Handicapped Association
P.O. Box 33150
Denver, CO 80233
Toll-Free Tel 1-800 369-7433
Tel (303) 452-1212
Fax (303) 252-4610
http://www.narha.org

Spruce Meadows
R.R. 9
Calgary, AB T2J 5G5
Tel (403) 974-4200
Fax (403) 974-4270
http://www.sprucemeadows.com
Host facility of major equestrian events.

The United States Combined Training Association
525 Old Waterford Road NW
Leesburg, VA 20176
Tel (703) 779-0440
E-mail < info@eventingusa.com>
http://www.eventingusa.com

United States Dressage Federation
P.O. Box 6669
Lincoln, NE 68506-0669
Tel (402) 434-8550
Fax (402) 434-8570
E-mail <usdressage@navix.net>
Governing body for equestrian sport.

United States Pony Clubs
4071 Iron Works Parkway
Lexington, KY 40511-8462
Tel (606) 254-7669
Fax (606) 233-4652
http://www.ponyclub.org

INTERNATIONAL

Association of British Riding Schools
Queens Chambers
38-40 Queen Street
Penzance
Cornwall TR18 4BH
United Kingdom

The British Horse Society
Stoneleigh Deer Park
Kenilworth
Warwickshire, CV8 2XZ
United Kingdom

British Equestrian Federation
National Agricultural Centre
Stoneleigh Park

Kenilworth
Warwickshire CV8 2RH
United Kingdom

**International Group for
Qualifications in Training
Horse & Rider
c/o The British Horse
Society**
Stoneleigh Deer Park
Kenilworth
Warwickshire, CV8 2XZ
United Kingdom

**Society of Master Saddlers
(UK) Ltd.**
Kettles Farm
Mickfield
Stowmarket
Suffolk IP14 6BY
United Kingdom

FURTHER READING

The following selection of
books and magazines are
particularly useful for novice
riders and horse owners.

BOOKS
*101 Arena Exercises: A
Ringside Guide for Horse &
Rider*, Cherry Hill, Storey
Books (1995)

*The Adventure Starts Here
...the Novice Amateur
Experience: A Beginners Guide
to Competitive Showing*, Carol
Lynn Pearce, Mayapple
Imaging (1996)

*The Affordable Horse: A Guide
to Low-Cost Ownership*,
Sharon B. Smith, IDG Books
Worldwide (1994)

*Basic Horse Care (Doubleday
Equestrian Library)*, Eleanor F.
Prince, Gaydell Collier
(Contributor), Main Street
Books (1989)

Beginning English Exercises,
Cherry Hill, Storey Books
(1998)

*Buying Your First Horse: A
Comprehensive Guide to
Preparing For, Finding and
Purchasing a Great Horse*,
Mary Guay and Donna
Schlinkert, White Papers
Press (1997)

Centered Riding, Sally Swift,
Jean McFarlane, Mike Noble,
St. Martins Press (1985)

The Encyclopedia of the Horse,
Elwyn Hartley Edwards,
Sharon Ralls Lemon, DK
Publishing (U.S.); Firefly
Books Ltd. (Canada) (1999)

*Equal to the Challenge:
Pioneering Women of Horse
Sports*, Jackie C. Burke, IDG
Books Worldwide (1997)

*The Horse—The Foot, Shoeing
and Lameness*, Julie Brega, J A
Allen & Co (1999)

*Horse Gaits, Balance and
Movement*, Susan E. Harris,
François Lemaire de Ruffieu,
IDG Books Worldwide
(1993)

*Horse Handling and Grooming:
A Step-by-Step Photographic
Guide to Mastering over 100
Horsekeeping Skills*, Cherry
Hill, Richard Klimesch,
Storey Books (1997)

*Horse Health Care: A Step-by-
Step Photographic Guide to
Mastering over 100
Horsekeeping Skills*, Cherry
Hill, Cherry, Richard
Klimesch, Storey Books
(1997)

*The Illustrated Guide to Horse
Tack: For the English Rider*,
Susan McBane, Gwen Steege
(Editor), Storey Books
(1996)

Improve Your Riding Skills,
Carolyn Henderson, Firefly
Books Ltd. (Canada); DK
Publishing (U.S.) (2000)

The Kingdom of the Horse,
Caroline Davis (Consultant
Editor), Firefly Books Ltd.
(1998)

*Anne Kursinski's Riding and
Jumping Clinic: A Step-By-Step
Course for Winning in the
Hunter and Jumper Rings*,
Anne Kursinski, Miranda
Lorraine (Contributor),
Doubleday (1995)

The Less-Than-Perfect Rider,
Caroline Davis, Lesley
Bayley, IDG Books
Worldwide (1994)

The Mind of the Horse, R.H.
Smythe, BookSales Inc.
(1997)

*Practical Horse and Pony
Nutrition*, Gillian McCarthy,
J A Allan & Co (1998)

Reading the Horse's Mind,
Jackie Budd, IDG Books
Worldwide (1996)

*Saddlery & Horse Equipment:
The Complete Illustrated Guide
to Riding Tack*, Sarah Muir,
Kit Houghton
(Photographer), Anness Pub
Ltd. (1999)

*The TV Vet Horse Book
(Recognition and Treatment of
Common Horse and Pony
Ailments)*, Eddie Straiton,
Diamond Farm Book
Publications (1987)

*The United States Pony Club
Guide to Conformation,
Movement and Soundness*,
Susan E. Harris, Ruth Ring
Harvie, United States Pony
Clubs, IDG Books
Worldwide (1997)

*The United States Pony Club
Manual of Horsemanship for
Beginners*, Susan E. Harris,
Ruth Ring Harvie, IDG
Books Worldwide (1994)

*The Way of the Horse: How to
See the World Through His
Eyes* (Howell Equestrian
Library), Jane Kidd (Editor),
IDG Books Worldwide
(1998)

The Whole Horse Catalog,
Steven D. Price, Barbara
Burn, David A. Spector,
Fireside (1998)

MAGAZINES
The Chronicle of the Horse
P.O. Box 46
Middleburg, VA 20118
Tel (540) 687-6341
Fax (540) 687-3937
For the horse lover.

The Corinthian-Horse Sport
P.O. Box 670
Aurora, ON L4G 4J9
Toll-Free 1-800-509-7428
Tel (905) 727-0107
Fax (905) 841-1530
*This publication's focus is
Canadian equestrian sports.*

Dressage and CT
P.O. Box 530
Unionville, PA 19375
Tel (610) 380-8977
Fax (610) 380-8304
E-mail <dressage@
equinesource.com>
*Covers the equestrian
disciplines of dressage and
combined.*

Dressage Today
656 Quince Orchard Road
Suite 600
Gaithersburg, MD 20878
Tel (301) 977-3900
Fax (301) 990-9015
*This publication's focus is
dressage.*

Equine Times
P.O. Box 8
Camden, MI 49232
Toll-Free 1-800-222-6336
Tel (517) 368-0365
Fax (517) 368-5131
For horse enthusiasts.

HorsePlay
656 Quince Orchard Road
Suite 600
Gaithersburg, MD 20878-
1409
Tel (301) 977-3900
Fax (301) 990-9015
*Regular features include Rider
Profiles, Training, and Horse
Care.*

Horsepower Magazine
P.O. Box 670
Aurora, ON L4G 4J9
Toll-Free 1-800-505-7428
Tel (905) 727-0107
Fax (905) 841-1530
E-mail <horsepower@
horsenet.com>
*Educational and safety articles
about horses for children aged
8-16.*

Horse Show
220 East 42nd Street
Suite 409
New York, NY 10017-5806
Tel (212) 972-2472
Fax (212) 983-7286
*Equestrian guide with regular
features such as Amateur
Perspective, Equestrian's
Bookshelf.*

Practical Horseman
P.O. Box 589
Unionville, PA
19375-0589
Tel (610) 380-8977
Fax (610) 380-8304
E-mail <prachorse@aol.com>
Focuses on English-style riding.

Riding
Green Shires Group Ltd
Telford Way
Kettering
North Hants
NN16 8UN
E-mail <publishing@
greenshires.com>
http:/www.ridingmagazine.
co.uk
*English magazine available on
subscription for horse owners
and riding enthusiasts.*

aids (signals to horse) 16, 18-26
    artificial 24-5
    natural 18-24

balance 16, 36
bedding 100, 106
bit 18, 33, 40
blankets 109
bridle, putting on 80-90
bucking, dealing with 92-3
buying a horse 98-104

canter 31, 71-7
    aids 74-5
    half-seat 73-4
    horse's movement 72
    rider's position 73-4
    speed 76
    types 72-3
classical riding 114
competing 11, 113-20
countryside, riding in 91-2
cross-country 116

dismounting 47
dressage 114, 115
driving 115

emergency stop 78
endurance riding 115
equipment, see tack
eventing 116
exercises 49, 50
    school 51-4

facial and body language,
    equine 31-2
falling off 13-14, 64
feeding 107-8
feet, cleaning 105

gallop 31
    horse's movement 73, 78
    rider's position 78
"giving" 24
glasses, wearing 15

gravity, center of 19-20
grooming 110-11

half-halt 24
halt 62
hands, use of 23
health problems, and riding 14-15
helmets 44, 45
horseball 116-17
hunting 117

illness 111-12
injuries, limiting risk of 13-14, 64
insurance 104
internal organs, equine 30
"letter system" 52
lunge lessons 41-2, 48-9

manège 52
martingales 25, 43
mounting 46-7
mouth and teeth care 111

napping, coping with 94

pasture, provision and care of 99, 105
paces, equine 31
polo and polocross 117-18
pony, definition of 49
posture, importance of 20-1, 29, 34

rearing, coping with 93
rein, changing the 54
reins, holding 60
riding alone 87-96
    coping with problems 92-5
riding instructor, compatibility
    39-41
riding lessons 12, 37-50
riding and pony clubs 101, 120
riding school, choosing 12, 38-9
riding wear 44-5
roads, riding on 90-1, 96

saddles 40, 57, 108

putting on 89
safety wear 44
seat 20-1, 22, 57, 58-9
skeleton, equine 29
snaffle bits 40
shoeing 100, 112
showing and showjumping 118
shying, coping with 95
sidesaddle 118-19
spurs 25
stabling 99-100, 105-6
stiffness and soreness 49
stirrups 40
    correct fit 46, 48
    position 59
    working without 63-4
stitch, coping with 70

tack 40, 43, 108
tacking up 88-90
transport 100
trot 65-70
    aids for 68-9
    horse's movement 66
    posting trot 66-8
    rider's position 66-8
    rising to 66-7
    sitting to 68
    speed 70
    types 66
turning, aids for 62-3

vaccinations 111
vaulting 119
veterinarians 100, 103-4
vision, equine 33
voice, use of 22-3

walk 31, 55-64
    aids for 60-2
    horse's movement in 57
    rider's position 58-9
    speed 64
    turning 62-3
    without stirrups 63-4
western riding 120
whips 24
worming 111

Picture credits

The publisher would like to thank the following for permission to reproduce their material. While every effort has been made to ensure this listing is correct, the publisher apologizes for any omissions.
Iain Burns: pp 1, 2, 3, 6-21, 26, 30, 33, 34, 37-39, 58-61, 69-71, 75-77, 79-85, 88 (t, b left), 90, 91 (l), 95-101, 104, 105, 107, 110 (t), 112, 113, 114 (t, r), 116, 118, 119, 120 (b), 122, 123
Bob Langrish: pp 25, 27, 46-48, 51, 54, 55, 63, 65, 87, 88 (b center and right), 89, 91 (c, r), 92-94, 103, 114 (l), 115, 120 (t), 121
Toggi and Champion, Finest Brands International, www.toggi.co.uk: pp 44-45
Paul L.E. Raper-Zullig: p 86
Shires Equestrian Products, Herefordshire, UK: pp 24, 40, 43, 102, 109, 110 (b)
Eugene Fleury: pp 28, 30, 31, 32, 33